THE FOUNTAINWELL DRAMA TEXTS

General Editors

T. A. DUNN

ANDREW GURR

JOHN HORDEN

A. NORMAN JEFFARES

R. L. C. LORIMER

Assistant General Editor

BRIAN W. M. SCOBIE

10

PHILIP MASSINGER

and

NATHAN FIELD

———

THE FATAL DOWRY

Edited by
T. A. DUNN

———

OLIVER & BOYD
EDINBURGH
1969

OLIVER AND BOYD LTD

Tweeddale Court
Edinburgh 1

First Published 1969

Hardback   05 0017187
Paperback   05 0017195

Printed in Great Britain by
Hazell Watson & Viney Ltd,
Aylesbury, Bucks

ACKNOWLEDGMENTS

This edition was prepared during a year spent as Visiting Professor in the University of Western Ontario. I would extend my grateful thanks to the University and the Department of English for making my work possible, and in particular to Professor Herbert Berry and Dr E. J. Devereux for much helpful advice. My thanks are also due to John Horden and Brian Scobie for supervision of this edition, for much kindness and encouragement, and for freely giving of their time and experience.

T. A. DUNN

Stirling
1 May 1968

ACKNOWLEDGMENTS

CONTENTS

CRITICAL INTRODUCTION   1

A NOTE ON THE TEXT   9

THE FATAL DOWRY   15

TEXTUAL NOTES   99

COMMENTARY   103

BIBLIOGRAPHY   109

GLOSSARY   111

CRITICAL INTRODUCTION

Although *The Fatal Dowry* was not published until 1632, it must have been written by 1620, in which year Nathan Field, one of its co-authors, died[1]. In this we are confirmed, moreover, by the nature of the collaboration. From the ease with which any reader can distinguish the contributions of the two authors, it is clear that the play is a genuine collaboration; it is not a revision by Massinger of an earlier work by Field. While it is not possible to set an exact date to the composition, the stylistic assurance of Massinger's contribution places it closer to *The Duke of Milan* (1621) than to earlier work, and, in the absence of external or any more positive internal evidence, 1619 would seem to be a likely date[2]. Although the 1632 entry of the play in the Stationers' Register describes it as having been licensed by Sir Henry Herbert, who did not become Master of the Revels until 1623, no other evidence of such licensing survives[3] and this statement must either be erroneous or refer to his relicensing of an old play prior to publication. The play belonged to the King's Men, in which company Field was one of the principal actors, and is clearly associated with the small group of plays Massinger wrote for them before moving across to the Queen's Men from 1625 to 1626[4].

Before writing *The Fatal Dowry* Field and Massinger had been friends and collaborators for a number of years. Their names have been linked in several collaborations with Fletcher on internal evidence[5],

---

[1] R. F. Brinkley, *Nathan Field, the Actor-Playwright*, in *Yale Studies in English*, LXXVII (1928), p. 153. The best brief account of Nathan Field is in G. E. Bentley, *The Jacobean and Caroline Stage*, III, pp. 299–302. Oxford (Oxford U.P.) 1956.

[2] C. L. Lockert, *The Fatal Dowry*, pp. 2–6. Lancaster, Penn. (New Era) 1918.

[3] F. G. Fleay in his *Biographical Chronicle of the English Drama* (London 1891). suggested that the lost play, *The Judge*, licensed by Herbert in 1627, was, in fact, *The Fatal Dowry*. Since both titles appear in later documents of the King's company, this is unlikely, however appropriate the title might be. See Bentley, *Jacobean Stage*, IV, pp. 784–5.

[4] T. A. Dunn, *Philip Massinger: The Man and the Playwright*, pp. 28–9. London (Nelson) 1957.

[5] As, for example, by Cyrus Hoy, "The Shares of Fletcher and his Collaborators in the Beaumont and Fletcher Canon", in *Studies in Bibliography*, XII (1959), XV (1962).

but they are positively and indissolubly united in one of the most famous theatrical documents we have. This is the famous "Tripartite Letter" of 1613, a mendicant epistle addressed by Field to the theatrical manager, Philip Henslowe, with postscripts by Daborne and Massinger: it asks him to advance them some money so that they could be bailed out of prison[6]. The letter shows that by that time they had collaborated with Fletcher in writing one play for Henslowe, and were then engaged in writing another. But *The Fatal Dowry* is the final and finest fruit of their collaboration.

By and large, it is a fairly simple matter to distinguish on stylistic grounds the main author of each scene, particularly since Massinger's voice (in extended passages at least) is unmistakable[7]. Field's speech-rhythms are much more naturalistic and less rhetorical. To him may be assigned the opening of II. II probably as far as line 173; Act III, with occasional touches of Massinger towards the end; and IV. I and v. I. The rest is by Massinger.

But it would be unwise to think because one of the authors was mainly responsible for a given scene that the other did not intervene. In any scene we might expect to find touches—words, phrases, even whole additional lines—contributed by the partner who was not responsible for the bulk of the writing. Throughout the play we can detect—or, at least, suspect—this happening, and it would be a bold scholar who would dare to assign to one or other author every line in such a work, since, by definition, a collaboration renders this difficult. We must not assume that the partners worked in isolation according to an agreed plan and story and merely cobbled together the final result. It would be only natural for each scene as completed to be discussed by both writers and for alterations to be incorporated in the final text. Moreover, it is always possible that occasional touches were added by Massinger long after Field's death, perhaps for a later production[8].

Similarly, we must not think that because Field was only directly responsible for writing about forty per cent of the lines his influence

---

[6] See W. W. Greg, *Henslowe Papers*, (1907) Article 68, the photograph in A. H. Cruickshank, *Philip Massinger*, opp. p. 4, and the transcript in Dunn, *Philip Massinger*, p. 15.

[7] For a full analysis of Massinger's style see Dunn, *Op. cit.*, Chapter 6.

[8] As, for example, when it was produced at the Cockpit on 3 February 1630/1. See Bentley, *Jacobean Stage*, I pp. 27–8.

upon the whole was negligible. The entire character of Young Novall, for example, lies in scenes by Field. Indeed, it is tempting to see something of the handsome young actor whose portrait hangs in Dulwich College in this direct ancestor of Rowe's "gallant, gay Lothario", this distant progenitor of Richardson's Lovelace. Certainly, it is true that, in intervals of acting and writing plays, Field managed to get himself involved in notoriously scandalous dealings with sundry ladies[9].

Young Novall is, of course, in some ways the most interesting character in the play. An unscrupulous and handsome lady-killer must always hold a certain attraction for an audience, gratifying, as he does, the romantic fantasies of both men and women. Certainly there is no moral justification to be presented in support of one who openly declares:

> Like a free wanton jennet i'th meddows,
> I looke about, and neigh, take hedge and ditch,
> Feed in my neighbours pastures, picke my choyce
> Of all their fair-maind-mares:[10]

even if his offences are today more likely to be considered venial than in 1620. Yet, if for no other reason, to be convincing in his appeal to Beaumelle he must appeal to us. This could hardly have been a task that lent itself to Massinger's high seriousness of approach: a hypocrite, or a double-dyed villain, is more in his line than a philanderer. But since he appears in II. II and dies in IV. II, Massinger had to give him only a very few lines in all, including the four remorseful lines he speaks as he faces his end. The rest is Field's, and much more lightly and colloquially written.

This fact, of course, is bound to contribute towards Young Novall's attractiveness. For, alone amongst the principal characters, he has none of the lengthy rhetorical speeches in involved periodic syntax which are so characteristic a feature of the Massinger scenes. It is this rhetorical predominance that is the most striking aspect of the play and renders it overwhelmingly forensic in tone.

Forensic drama is, indeed, Massinger's speciality. There is none of his plays that does not have its trial, its judgment or its pleading scene or does not frequently lapse into the presentation of static debate. *The Fatal Dowry*, in Massinger scenes, is no exception. Both the first and

---

[9] See Bentley, *Jacobean Stage*, III p. 301.
[10] *The Fatal Dowry*, hereafter cited as *F.D.*, IV. I. 80–3.

the last acts of the play consist of elaborate and detailed trial scenes with the main characters engaged in lengthy rhetorical pleas, and IV. IV comprises the debate of Charalois and Beaumelle and her "judgment" and condemnation by her own father. One third of the play, in fact, is made up of this formal confrontation, and much of the rest is made up of similar purely "rhetorical action", in scenes of suasion which, though not so formally epideictic as the trials proper, hinge upon argument—as in Romont's unsuccessful bid to persuade Charalois of Beaumelle's fickleness or in the passage at the beginning of Act III in which Bellapert convinces Young Novall of the advantages of making love to a married woman.

But drama that is forensic is none the less drama, and action that is verbal is none the less theatrically effective. Dramatists from Shakespeare to Shaw have demonstrated this, and almost nightly the television theatre of today presents us with evidence of the fascination the trial setting holds for the public. The presentation of debate in *The Fatal Dowry* is made with firmness and stylistic power. It cannot fail to grip an audience, intellectually if not emotionally, and to a certain extent reflects the increased interest of the Jacobean audience in intellectualisation that marches with the move away from the popular theatre to the private houses. To debate such topics as infidelity and its punishment, to perform a dramatic action and then to discuss it, is to move away from the emotional involvement called for by such concrete exemplification as we find in, say, *Othello* towards a more Brechtian detachment in which the concern is with the subject debated rather than with living, suffering human beings. When characters are presenting the case for themselves rather than mediating their own existence to us their gestures tend to be those of wooden automata. However, in the greatest trial scenes in drama the audience is gripped not alone by a delight in the argument for oratory's sake but has a dual involvement in that they also care what happens to the characters.

Had the characters preserved throughout the play the woodenness they tend towards in the trial scenes alone, then we would indeed find it difficult to involve ourselves with them. But, of course, they do not. The freer, middle parts of the play, in which Field, with his more naturalistic dialogue, was concerned, come in between. Thus, by the time we reach the great forensic passages at the end, we are able to operate in the area of dual involvement and to care about the dilemmas of the characters as well as about the arguments they present.

This is not, perhaps, so true of the first part of the play, up to the marriage of Charalois with Beaumelle. Up to the end of II. II the character of Charalois seems largely a cardboard cut-out of a noble soldier in a grossly unfair, not to mention rather far-fetched, situation. The material itself, however, and its unusual nature, is interesting enough to carry us into the play, but it must be recognised that the difficulty of involving ourselves with the characters at this point does increase the feeling we have that this first part of the play forms in itself an almost self-contained action. That we should be presented with a full account of the circumstances leading up to the marriage of Charalois with Beaumelle, and that this marriage, infidelity within which forms the main action of the play, should not take place until the end of Act II, looks like a defect in plotting. After all, when *Othello* begins, Othello and Desdemona have just married and the concentration throughout the play is upon this marriage disrupted by jealousy. When Nicholas Rowe made an adaptation of the play (*The Fair Penitent*, 1703), he perhaps tacitly recognised its defective plotting and took Act III as his starting-point.

However, because of the situation in which we find him and because of the legal gravity of his address, by the time of the marriage we have received a very firm impression of the character of Charalois. He is courageous, noble and deeply-engrossed in concern for his honour. His *pietas* and *gravitas*, as displayed to us, lend him an authority which we know will not readily be shaken by jealousy. Nor, as the action unfolds, is it. This is no pale shadow of Othello, easily moved to suspicion. He does not demand, but he does receive, ocular proof of Beaumelle's infidelity. And once he has this proof, he proceeds, not through hysterical tantrums but with judicial deliberation, to an exaction which vindicates his honour. That he is mistaken in acting this way, that one should not be a judge in one's own cause, that:

> how just soever
> Our reasons are to remedy our wrongs,
> We are yet to leave them to their will and power,
> That to that purpose have authority[11]

is the moral of the story, and the character of Charalois is closely adapted to this end. He is patiently and definitively the sort of man who would inevitably act in this particular way.

[11] *F.D.*, v. II. 392–5.

The guilty action of Beaumelle and Young Novall is not nearly so clearly motivated. The easy morality of Beaumelle's household and maidservants is established in ii. ii, but Beaumelle's honour itself is not imputed—rather the contrary. She it is who would "meete love and marriage both at once"[12]; she it is who confronts Bellapert's hedonistic philosophy with "But there is honor, wench"[13] It is briefly made clear that she is strongly attracted by Young Novall's courtesies, but, when she is given by her father to Charalois, there is no hint that she surrenders unwillingly:

> CHARALOIS.   Faire *Beaumelle*, can you love me?
> BEAUMELLE.   Yes, my Lord.[14]

When Young Novall steps forward to her, her reply indicates that she is at least determined to act honourably:

> Oh servant, vertue strengthen me.
> The presence blowes round my affections vane:
> You will undoe me, if you speake againe.[15]

Thus the adultery of the second part of the play is just barely adumbrated by the end of Act II.

In the same way, Act IV concludes almost as finally as Act V of *Othello*. The adultery has been discovered, Young Novall killed and then Beaumelle is slain as the climax of the highly dramatic scene in which the blindfold Rochfort has condemned his own daughter. The purpose of Act V is more moral than dramatic and deals with the consequences of the preceding action.

But there is a sense in which the whole drama is a moral one. The area of the play is that of abstractions of human relationships. Charalois is noble and honourable, slow to anger and cool and legalistic in exacting his penalties. Beaumelle is a weak, not a sinful, wife, who knows full well the better way yet takes the worse. Romont is the honourable and blunt soldier, the true friend, opposed to Young Novall, the courtier, whose view of honour is of something of no virtue or value, who refuses, as in iv. i. 130ff., to fight upon a point of honour. Pontalier will fight honourably for his corrupt master. Rochfort distinguishes, and is crushed to pieces, between the upper and nether millstones of his duties as a parent and his position as a

---

[12] *F.D.*, ii. ii. 55.   [13] *F.D.*, ii. ii. 42.   [14] *F.D.*, ii. ii. 345–6.
[15] *F.D.*, ii. ii. 377–9.

judge. Loyalty and trust, and their opposites, form the antithetical themes of the play.

To express these themes, the play centres round the idea of *courtesy*. Charalois dismisses Romont's report that Beaumelle is being too familiar with Young Novall as describing "Meere complement and courtship"[15]. Young Novall, who is constantly referred to as Beaumelle's *servant*, is so in an honourable way—or so Charalois, who can think little ill of others, would say. A lady is free and honourable and is owed such courtesy by her servant. But that the word *servant* has specific connotation and *courtesy* is more than an outward show of formal politeness is frequently made plain. As Bellapert says:

> In this word courtesy, we that are gamesters point at
> The sport direct, where not alone the lover
> Brings his Artillery, but uses it.[16]

The chivalric idea of courtesy and service, where the lover serves his mistress chastely and honourably, persists in the military caste of Charalois and Romont, is found even in Pontalier, and is reflected in the moral-legal judgments of the play. But in the world of courtly dalliance, the world of Young Novall and his associates, it has become a dead letter. That Jacobean society should concern itself with a play which discusses these issues is significant: there are many similar plays in the Fletcherian school of drama. That these issues, or something very like them, are also alive for audiences today is undeniable. The blend in *The Fatal Dowry* of Massinger's rhetorical eloquence, and its carefully-articulated periodic sentences, with Field's more nervous and realistic style[17], could appeal powerfully to a modern audience as a counterbalance to such blood-soaked, action-packed drama of infidelity in personal relationships as we find in Webster— which alone outside Shakespeare finds its way into our theatres as representative of Jacobean tragedy.

Although *The Fatal Dowry* was still a viable property when in 1681 it was reassigned to Benjamin Thrale[18], and appears in January 1668/9 in a list of plays formerly acted at Blackfriars and now

---

[15] *F.D.*, III. I. 521.   [16] *F.D.*, III. I. 38–40.

[17] See Romont's speech, v. II. 118–133, for a fine example of his handling of a complex sentence. In both prose and verse, IV. I illustrates Field's more rapid, naturalistic interchange.

[18] See below, p. 10.

allowed of to the King's Company[19], its stage-history is mostly in an adapted form. Rowe's *The Fair Penitent* (1703, and many later editions), which is based on it, was one of the most popular plays of the eighteenth century, and later, closer adaptations are found in Aaron Hill's *The Insolvent, or Filial Piety* (pub. 1758)[20], and in those by J. S. Knowles (pub. 1825) and R. L. Sheil (presented at Drury Lane)[21]. There have been no productions in modern times.

[19] *The London Stage 1660–1800, Part 1: 1660–1700*, ed. W. Van Lennep, p. 152. Carbondale, Ill. (Southern Illinois U.P.) 1965.

[20] Allardyce Nicoll, *A History of English Drama 1660–1900*, II, p. 438; III, pp. 113 and 268. Cambridge (Cambridge U.P.) 1955. *The London Stage 1660–1800, Part 4: 1747–1776*, ed. G. W. Stone, Jr., II, pp. 651–2, 655. Carbondale, Ill. (Southern Illinois U.P.) 1962. See also, J. F. Kermode, "A Note on the History of *The Fatal Dowry* in the Eighteenth Century", *N. & Q.*, CXCII (3 May 1947), pp. 186–7; and *Annals of English Drama 975–1700*, ed. A. Harbage, rev. S. Schoenbaum, pp. 205–6. London (Methuen) 1964.

[21] See Nicoll, *History of English Drama*, IV, 339 and 610.

A NOTE ON THE TEXT

There is only one early edition of *The Fatal Dowry*: a Quarto printed by John Norton for Francis Constable and dated 1632[1]. It had been entered in the Stationers' Register to Constable on 30 March 1632 (where it is described as having been licensed by Sir Henry Herbert)[2], and later entries in the Register occur on 17 February 1648, when the administrators of the estate of Constable's widow transferred it to R. Thrale[3], and in April 1681, when Thrale's widow transferred it to B. Thrale[4].

The title-page describes the play "As it hath beene often Acted at the Private House in Blackefryers, by his Majesties Servants", and as "Written by P.M. and N.F.". There is no doubt that the authors are Philip Massinger and Nathan Field.

The collation of the Quarto is A[2], B-L[4], all 42 leaves being un-numbered. The Title is on A1 recto, a list of Dramatis Personae on A1 verso and the four songs appear on A2 recto and verso.

Greg records the locations of 25 copies[5], and, unlike certain other plays by Massinger[6], none appears to contain the author's manuscript corrections. As was normal practice, however, sheets were corrected in press, and a number of minor press-variants may be found.

There are fairly positive indications that the copy Norton's

---

[1] S.T.C. 17646. W. W. Greg, *A Bibliography of the English Printed Drama to the Restoration*, 4 vols, No 464. London (Bibliographical Society) 1939–59.

[2] Greg, *Op. cit.*, vol. I, pp. 41. No record of this licensing has survived, and, of course, Herbert did not become Master of the Revels until July 1623. See J. Q. Adams, *The Dramatic Records of Sir Henry Herbert*, p. 38 n. 3, where he records that Malone specifically notes that there was no mention of *The Fatal Dowry* in the original office-book. Yale (Yale U.P.) 1917.

[3] No 11 in a list of 20 titles. Greg, *Op. cit.*, p. 58.

[4] No 24 in a list of 42 titles, registered by an assignment bearing the date 28 March 1681. Greg, *Op. cit.*, p. 74.

[5] Greg's list is representative, not comprehensive.

[6] *E.g.* The Dyce copy of *The Duke of Milan*. Possibly also *The Bondman, The Emperor of the East, The Renegado, The Roman Actor*, and (in part) *The Picture*. See W. W. Greg, *The Library*, IV (1923), p. 207, I (1924), pp. 59–91, J. E. Gray, *The Library*, V (1950), pp. 132–9, and A. K. McIlwraith, *The Library*, VI (1951), pp. 213–16. Also, A. H. Cruickshank, *Philip Massinger*, Appendix XIX, pp. 215–23.

compositor had before him in setting the play was a manuscript in
two hands, corresponding to the parts written by Massinger and Field
respectively. To show this conclusively would require a detailed
statistical study comparing the spelling of common words and mor-
phemes from the two suggested hands, drawn both from this play
and from undisputed work by the two authors; and the hazardous
tedium of such an investigation need not be elaborated upon. However,
perhaps two examples of unusual words will suffice to add weight to
this suggestion: *banquerout* (bankrupt) appears twice in passages by
Massinger (I. I. 154, I. II. 100), but appears as *bankerupt* in II. II. 300,
equally certainly by Field; and *Dijon* appears thus in Massinger
scenes (I. II, II. I), but as *Dijum* and *Digum* in a Field scene (II. II. 70,
349). Moreover, the absence in Massinger's portions of certain abb-
reviated forms (*e.g.* i'th', o'th') which have been shown to be uncommon
in his work[7], combined with their presence in portions which can be
definitely assigned to Field, suggests that the copy was indeed in the
hands of the two authors. On balance, the interpolation of a scribal
transcript seems unlikely and would probably have produced a greater
degree of normalisation between the contributions of the two authors
than we find here. The fact that the compositor was setting from the
holograph of Massinger and Field gives the Quarto considerable
authority.

However, a third hand, not that of either of the authors, may be
detected at work in the stage-directions. Most of the stage-directions
are clearly authorial and are printed interlineally, but a number of
additional directions have been printed marginally. Their positioning,
sometimes inexact, suggests strongly that they appeared as marginal
additions to the manuscript, and the spelling of characters' names
(*e.g. Beaumely* at III. I. 60, IV. II. 104, and *Aymiere* at IV. II. 36) or the
substitution of descriptions for names (*e.g. Mrs.*, and *Daug.* at II. II.
164), makes it clear that they were not inserted by one of the authors.
These directions are "descriptive" rather than "imperative" in form
and do not have the definitely theatrical flavour of the interesting
directions added to *The City Madam*, so it is likely that they were
inserted for the benefit of the reader. They might, of course, have
been added in the theatre, and in a play so uncomplicated in its

[7] Cyrus Hoy, "The Shares of Fletcher and his Collaborators in the Beaumont
and Fletcher Canon", in *S.B.*, VIII–IX, XI–XV (1955–62).

"business" such a manuscript could well have formed the prompt-copy; but on the whole the impression is of an authorial fair-copy carefully prepared for the press.

Since the printer's copy varied between two hands, there is little that can be said about the setting of the first edition without a per-adventure. Two compositors seem to have been at work: one who produces what could be described as "conservative" and more individualistic forms (*e.g. comminge, sonne, mannage, fauor, conuayance, coorse, wayte*) and who is less likely to use apostrophes in participles (*e.g. prayd, hangd, damnd, honord, deferd*) and words like *orecome* than the other, and a second who seems more "modern" and normalises his spellings much more. It is an open question which is more likely to preserve authorial forms. They produced a text in which there is little corruption—and consequently little of textual interest arising from purely bibliographical considerations. The few cruxes are considered in the Textual Notes, but most emendation that has been necessary has been of simple literal errors where the true reading is so obvious that the emendation may be recorded without further comment.

The play was reprinted in all the collected editions of Massinger's work[8], but the only separate edition, other than the Quarto, is that published in 1918 by C. L. Lockert[9]. Lockert does not tell us which copy he used, but it is clear that it contained an uncorrected state of the inner forme of sig. L not to be found in the copies which have been collated for this edition[10]. His edition is a reprint of the Q1 in all accidentals but not in pagination. He corrects the metrical alignment where he considers it necessary, and while he records variations in subsequent editions he gives no collation of copies of the Quarto itself.

The present edition is based on a collation of three copies: Folger Shakespeare Library (S.T.C. 17646 copy 1), British Museum (644.e.85) and the copy in the Library of Congress. Variants from subsequent editions have not been recorded except where necessary for purposes of discussion, but have been given from Lockert's edition where the evidence suggests he was reading from uncorrected sheets.

Throughout, "long s", and the complementary letters ("i" and "j", "u" and "v", and "w" and "vv") have been normalised in accordance

[8] See Bibliography, p. 107.   [9] Lancaster, Pa. (New Era) 1918.
[10] See, for example, v. ii. 181.

with modern usage, except that in the Textual Notes the complementary letters have, where necessary, been rendered as in the original. Ampersands have been silently expanded throughout and numerals occurring in the paraphernalia have been altered to words.

The metrical alignment in verse is given exactly as in the First Edition, each line (complete or incomplete) being allotted one number, except that the songs have been corrected. Prose, however, has been set continuously with no attempt to represent the original lineation.

Otherwise than as stated above, in the *Text Proper (i.e.* all utterances by characters) the accidentals of the first edition have been reproduced. Any departure from the original punctuation has been recorded in the Textual Notes: for the most part this has comprised supplying or correcting punctuation at the end of lines[11], but on rare occasions punctuation within the line has been supplied or corrected where it is defective in a way that would interrupt the sense even for a reader accustomed to the vagaries of seventeenth-century practice. Similarly, lower-case initials have been replaced by capitals at the beginning of lines of verse where necessary. However, any departure whatsoever from the copy in the Text Proper has been recorded.

Slightly more liberty has been taken with the *Paraphernalia (i.e.* stage-directions, characters' names, and so on). All the names of characters have been regularised in the spelling in which they most commonly appear in the first edition and have been given in full in capitals and small capitals. Since the text usually makes the action clear, it has been necessary to add only a few additional stage-directions, and to expand only a few existing ones. These additions are rendered in pointed brackets. Locations provided by later editors are ignored. The few songs, originally printed separately in the half-sheet A, are inserted into the text in the proper places. Scene headings have been regularised silently, although those supplied editorially are given in pointed brackets.

Textual Notes are given in two places: those recording variants which significantly affect the meaning of the passage are set as footnotes on the relevant text pages; all others are gathered in the section at the back of the book.

The aim throughout has been to render a text that, purged of

---

[11] As, for example, where a question-mark has appeared for an exclamation-mark, a common, but unsystematised, Jacobean practice.

obscurities and misprints, is as close as possible to what John Norton intended to produce in 1632, presented in a setting acceptable to the reader or student interested in the seventeenth-century drama who wishes to get as close to the original as possible without the interposition of unacknowledged editorial conjecture or modernisation.

DRAMATIS PERSONAE

CHARALOIS

ROMONT

CHARMI

ROCHFORT

DU CROYE

NOVALL SENIOR

LILADAM

YOUNG NOVALL

BEAUMONT

PONTALIER

MALOTIN

AYMER

PAGE

BEAUMELLE

FLORIMELL

BELLAPERT

THREE CREDITORS, ADVOCATES, PRESIDENTS, OFFICERS, JAYLOR, PRIEST, CAPTAINS, SOLDIERS, TAYLOR, BARBER, *and* PERFUMER

ACT I

SCENE I

Enter CHARALOIS *with a paper*, ROMONT, CHARMI.

CHARMI.   Sir, I may move the Court to serve your will,
But therein shall both wrong you and my selfe.
ROMONT.   Why thinke you so sir?
CHARMI.   'Cause I am familiar
With what will be their answere: they will say,   5
Tis against law, and argue me of Ignorance
For offering them the motion.
ROMONT.   You know not, Sir,
How in this cause they may dispence with Law,
And therefore frame not you their answere for them,   10
But doe your parts.
CHARMI.   I love the cause so well,
As I could runne, the hazard of a checke for't.
ROMONT.   From whom?
CHARMI.   Some of the bench, that watch to give it,   15
More then to doe the office that they sit for:
But give me (sir) my fee.
ROMONT.   Now you are Noble.
CHARMI.   I shall deserve this better yet, in giving
My Lord some counsell, (if he please to heare it)   20
Then I shall doe with pleading.
ROMONT.   What may it be, sir?
CHARMI.   That it would please his Lordship, as the Presidents,
And Counsaylors of Court come by, to stand
Heere, and but shew your selfe, and to some one   25
Or two, make his request: there is a minute
When a mans presence speakes in his owne cause,
More then the tongues of twenty advocates.
ROMONT.   I have urg'd that.

Enter ROCHFORT: DU CROYE.

CHARMI.   Their Lordships here are comming,   30

I must goe get me a place, you'l finde me in Court,
And at your service.

Exit CHARMI.

ROMONT.   Now put on your Spirits.

⟨ROMONT *urges* CHARLOIS *to speak while* DU
CROYE *and* ROCHFORT *converse together.*⟩

DU CROYE.   The ease that you prepare your selfe, my Lord,
In giving up the place you hold in Court,
Will prove (I feare) a trouble in the State,   35
And that no slight one.

ROCHFORT.   Pray you sir, no more.

ROMONT.   Now sir, lose not this offerd meanes: their lookes
Fixt on you, with a pittying earnestnesse,
Invite you to demand their furtherance   40
To your good purpose.—This such a dulnesse
So foolish and untimely as—

DU CROYE.   You know him?

ROCHFORT.   I doe, and much lament the sudden fall   45
Of his brave house. It is young *Charloyes.*
Sonne to the Marshall, from whom he inherits
His fame and vertues onely.

ROMONT.   Ha, they name you.

DU CROYE.   His father died in prison two daies since.   50

ROCHFORT.   Yes, to the shame of this ungratefull State;
That such a Master in the art of warre,
So noble, and so highly meriting,
From this forgetfull Country, should, for want
Of meanes to satisfie his creditors,   55
The summes he tooke up for the generall good,
Meet with an end so infamous.

ROMONT.   Dare you ever hope for like oportunity?

DU CROYE.   My good Lord!

ROCHFORT.   My wish bring comfort to you.   60

DU CROYE.   The time calls us.

ROCHFORT.   Good morrow Colonell.

Exeunt ROCHFORT, DU CROYE.

ROMONT.   This obstinate spleene,
You thinke becomes your sorrow, and sorts wel

With your blacke suits: but grant me wit, or judgement,   65
And by the freedome of an honest man,
And a true friend to boote, I sweare 'tis shamefull.
And therefore flatter not your selfe with hope,
Your sable habit, with the hat and cloake,
No, though the ribons helpe, have power to worke'em   70
To what you would: for those that had no eyes,
To see the great acts of your father, will not,
From any fashion sorrow can put on,
Bee taught to know their duties.
CHARALOIS.   If they will not,   75
They are too old to learne, and I too young
To give them counsell, since if they partake
The understanding, and the hearts of men,
They will prevent my words and teares: if not,
What can perswasion, though made eloquent   80
With griefe, worke upon such as have chang'd natures
With the most savage beast? Blest, blest be ever
The memory of that happy age, when justice
Had no gards to keepe off wrongd innocence,
From flying to her succours, and in that   85
Assurance of redresse: where now (*Romont*)
The damnd, with more ease may ascend from Hell,
Then we arive at her. One Cerberus there
Forbids the passage, in our Courts a thousand,
As lowd, and fertyle headed, and the Client   90
That wants the sops, to fill their ravenous throats,
Must hope for no accesse: why should I then
Attempt impossibilities: you friend, being
Too well acquainted with my dearth of meanes,
To make my entrance that way?   95
ROMONT.   Would I were not.
But Sir, you have a cause, a cause so just,
Of such necessitie, not to be deferd,
As would compell a mayde, whose foot was never
Set ore her fathers threshold, nor within   100
The house where she was borne ever spake word,
Which was not ushered with pure virgin blushes,
To drowne the tempest of a pleaders tongue,

And force corruption to give back the hire
It tooke against her: let examples move you.   105
You see great men in birth, esteeme and fortune,
Rather then lose a scruple of their right,
Fawne basely upon such, whose gownes put off,
They would disdaine for Servants.
CHARALOIS.   And to these can I become a suytor?   110
ROMONT.   Without losse,
Would you consider, that to gaine their favors,
Our chastest dames put off their modesties,
Soldiers forget their honors, usurers
Make sacrifice of Gold, poets of wit,   115
And men religious, part with fame, and goodnesse?
Be therefore wonne to use the meanes, that may
Advance your pious ends.
CHARALOIS.   You shall orecome.
ROMONT.   And you receive the glory, pray you now practise.   120
'Tis well.

Enter NOVALL SENIOR, LILADAM, *and three* CREDITORS.

CHARALOIS.   Not looke on me!
ROMONT.   You must have patience—Offer't againe.
CHARALOIS.   And be againe contemn'd?
NOVALL SENIOR.   I know whats to be done.   125
FIRST CREDITOR.   And that your Lordship
Will please to do your knowledge, we offer, first
Our thankefull hearts heere, as a bounteous earnest
To what we will adde.
NOVALL SENIOR.   One word more of this   130
I am your enemie. Am I a man
Your bribes can worke on? ha?
LILADAM.   Friends, you mistake
The way to winne my Lord, he must not heare this,
But I, as one in favour, in his sight,   135
May harken to you for my profit. Sir,
I pray heare em.
NOVALL SENIOR.   Tis well.
LILADAM.   Observe him now.

NOVALL SENIOR. Your cause being good, and your pro- 140
ceedings so,
Without corruption; I am your friend,
Speake your desires.
SECOND CREDITOR. Oh, they are charitable,
The Marshall stood ingag'd unto us three,
Two hundred thousand crownes, which by his death 145
We are defeated of. For which great losse
We ayme at nothing but his rotten flesh,
Nor is that cruelty.
FIRST CREDITOR. I have a sonne,
That talkes of nothing but of Gunnes and Armors, 150
And sweares hee'll be a soldier, tis an humor
I would divert him from, and I am told
That if I minister to him in his drinke
Powder, made of this banquerout Marshalls bones,
Provided that the carcase rot above ground, 155
'T will cure his foolish frensie.
NOVALL SENIOR. You shew in it
A fathers care. I have a sonne my selfe,
A fashionable Gentleman and a peacefull:
And but I am assur'd he's not so given, 160
He should take of it too. Sir, what are you?
CHARALOIS. A Gentleman.
NOVALL SENIOR. So are many that rake dunghills.
If you have any suit, move it in Court.
I take no papers in corners. 165
ROMONT. Yes as the matter may be carried, and hereby
To mannage the convayance—Follow him.

Exit NOVALL SENIOR, CHARALOIS, *and* ADVOCATES.

LILADAM. You are rude. I say, he shall not passe.
ROMONT. You say so.
On what assurance? 170
For the well cutting of his Lordships cornes,
Picking his toes, or any office else
Neerer to basenesse!
LILADAM. Looke upon mee better,

Are these the ensignes of so coorse a fellow?   175
  Be well advis'd.
ROMONT.   Out, rogue, do not I know,   *Kicks him*
  These glorious weedes spring from the sordid dunghill
  Of thy officious basenesse? wert thou worthy
  Of any thing from me, but my contempt,   180
  I would do more then this, more, you Court-spider.
LILADAM.   But that this man is lawlesse; he should find
  That I am valiant.
FIRST CREDITOR.   If your eares are fast,
  Tis nothing. Whats a blow or two? as much—   185
SECOND CREDITOR.   These chastisements, as usefull are as
  frequent
  To such as would grow rich.
ROMONT.   Are they so Rascals? I wil be-friend you then.
FIRST CREDITOR.   Beare witnesse, Sirs.
LILADAM.   Trueth, I have borne my part already, friends.   190
  In the Court you shall have more.

                                    Exit ⟨LILADAM⟩.

ROMONT.   I know you for
  The worst of spirits, that strive to rob the tombes
  Of what is their inheritance, from the dead.
  For usurers, bred by a riotous peace: 195
  That hold the Charter of your wealth and freedome,
  By being Knaves and Cuckolds that ne're prayd,
  But when you feare the rich heires will grow wise,
  To keepe their Lands out of your parchment toyles;
  And then, the Divell your father's cald upon,   200
  To invent some wayes of *Luxury* ne're thought on.
  Be gone, and quickly, or Ile leave no roome
  Upon your forhead for your hornes to sprowt on;
  Without a murmure, or I will undoe you;
  For I will beate you honest.   205
FIRST CREDITOR.   Thrift forbid.
  We will beare this, rather then hazard that.

                                    Exit CREDITORS.

Enter CHARALOIS.

ROMONT.   I am some-what eas'd in this yet.

CHARALOIS.   (Onely friend)
  To what vaine purpose do I make my sorrow,   210
  Wayte on the triumph of their cruelty?
  Or teach their pride from my humilitie,
  To thinke it has orecome? They are determin'd
  What they will do: and it may well become me,
  To robbe them of the glory they expect   215
  From my submisse intreaties.
ROMONT.   Thinke not so, Sir,
  The difficulties that you incounter with,
  Will crowne the undertaking—Heaven! you weepe:
  And I could do so too, but that I know,   220
  Theres more expected from the sonne and friend
  Of him, whose fatall losse now shakes our natures,
  Then sighs, or teares, (in which a village nurse
  Or cunning strumpet, when her knave is hangd,
  May overcome us.) We are men (young Lord)   225
  Let us not do like women. To the Court,
  And there speake like your birth: wake sleeping justice,
  Or dare the Axe. This is a way will sort
  With what you are. I call you not to that
  I will shrinke from my selfe, I will deserve   230
  Your thankes, or suffer with you—O how bravely
  That sudden fire of anger shewes in you!
  Give fuell to it, since you are on a shelfe,
  Of extreme danger suffer like your selfe.

Exeunt.

⟨SCENE II⟩

Enter ROCHFORT, NOVALL SENIOR, CHARMI,
DU CROYE, ADVOCATES, BEAUMONT, *and*
OFFICERS *and three* CREDITORS.

DU CROYE.   Your Lordship's seated. May this meeting prove
  Prosperous to us, and to the general good of *Burgundy.*
NOVALL SENIOR.   Speake to the poynt.
DU CROYE.   Which is,
  With honour to dispose the place and power   5

Of primier President, which this reverent man
Grave *Rochfort*, (whom for honours sake I name)
Is purpos'd to resigne a place, my Lords,
In which he hath with such integrity,
Perform'd the first and best parts of a Judge,   10
That as his life transcends all faire examples
Of such as were before him in *Dijon*,
So it remaines to those that shall succeed him,
A President they may imitate, but not equall.

ROCHFORT.   I may not sit to heare this.   15
DU CROYE.   Let the love
And thankfulnes we are bound to pay to goodnesse,
In this o'recome your modestie.
ROCHFORT.   My thankes
For this great favour shall prevent your trouble.   20
The honourable trust that was impos'd
Upon my weaknesse, since you witnesse for me,
It was not ill discharg'd, I will not mention.
Nor now, if age had not depriv'd me of
The little strength I had to governe well,   25
The Province that I undertooke, forsake it.
NOVALL SENIOR.   That we could lend you of our yeeres!
DU CROYE.   Or strength.
NOVALL SENIOR.   Or as you are, perswade you to continue
The noble exercise of your knowing judgement.   30
ROCHFORT.   That may not be, nor can your Lordships goodnes,
Since your imployments have confer'd upon me
Sufficient wealth, deny the use of it,
And though old age, when one foot's in the grave,
In many, when all humors else are spent   35
Feeds no affection in them, but desire
To adde height to the mountaine of their riches:
In me it is not so, I rest content
With the honours, and estate I now possesse,
And that I may have liberty to use,   40
What Heaven still blessing my poore industry,
Hath made me Master of: I pray the Court
To ease me of my burthen, that I may
Employ the small remainder of my life,

In living well, and learning how to dye so.   45

Enter ROMONT, *and* CHARALOIS.

ROMONT.   See sir, our Advocate.
DU CROYE.   The Court intreats,
  Your Lordship will be pleased to name the man,
  Which you would have your successor, and in me,
  All promise to confirme it.   50
ROCHFORT.   I embrace it,
  As an assurance of their favour to me,
  And name my Lord *Novall.*
DU CROYE.   The Court allows it.
ROCHFORT.   But there are suters waite heere, and their causes   55
  May be of more necessity to be heard,
  And therefore wish that mine may be defer'd,
  And theirs have hearing.
DU CROYE.   If your Lordship please
  To take the place, we will proceed.   60
CHARMI.   The cause
  We come to offer your Lordships censure,
  Is in it selfe so noble, that it needs not
  Or Rhetorique in me that plead, or favour
  From your grave Lordships, to determine of it.   65
  Since to the prayse of your impartiall justice
  (Which guilty, nay condemn'd men, dare not scandall)
  It will erect a trophy of your mercy
  With, married to that, Justice.
NOVALL SENIOR.   Speake to the cause.   70
CHARMI.   I will, my Lord: to say, the late dead Marshall
  The father of this young Lord heere, my Clyent,
  Hath done his Country great and faithfull service,
  Might taske me of impertinence to repeate,
  What your grave Lordships cannot but remember.   75
  He in his life, become indebted to
  These thriftie men, I will not wrong their credits,
  By giving them the attributes they now merit,
  And fayling by the fortune of the warres,
  Of meanes to free himselfe, from his ingagements,   80
  He was arrested, and for want of bayle

Imprisond at their suite, and not long after
With losse of liberty ended his life.
And though it be a *Maxime* in our Lawes,
All suites dye with the person, these mens malice   85
In death find matter for their hate to worke on,
Denying him the decent Rytes of buriall,
Which the sworne enemies of the Christian faith
Grant freely to their slaves: may it therefore please
Your Lordships, so to fashion your decree,   90
That what their crueltie doth forbid, your pittie
May give allowance to.
NOVALL SENIOR.   How long have you Sir practis'd in Court?
CHARMI.   Some twenty yeeres, my Lord.
NOVALL SENIOR.   By your grosse ignorance it should appeare,   95
   Not twentie dayes.
CHARMI.   I hope I have given no cause in this, my Lord—
NOVALL SENIOR.   How dare you move the Court,
   To the dispensing with an Act confirmd
   By Parlament, to the terror of all banquerouts?   100
   Go home, and with more care peruse the Statutes:
   Or the next motion savoring of this booldnesse,
   May force you to leape (against your will)
   Over the place you plead at.
CHARMI.   I foresaw this.   105
ROMONT.   Why does your Lordship thinke, the moving of
   A cause more honest then this Court had ever
   The honor to determine, can deserve
   A checke like this?
NOVALL SENIOR.   Strange boldnes!   110
ROMONT.   Tis fit freedome:
   Or do you conclude, an advocate cannot hold
   His credit with the Judge, unlesse he study
   His face more then the cause for which he pleades?
CHARMI.   Forbeare.   115
ROMONT.   Or cannot you, that have the power
   To qualifie the rigour of the Lawes
   When you are pleased, take a little from
   The strictnesse of your sowre decrees, enacted
   In favor of the greedy creditors   120

Against the orethrowne debter?

NOVALL SENIOR.   Sirra, you that prate
Thus sawcily, what are you?

ROMONT.   Why Ile tell you,
Thou purple-colour'd man, I am one to whom   125
Thou owest the meanes thou hast of sitting there
A corrupt Elder.

CHARMI.   Forbeare.

ROMONT.   The nose thou wear'st, is my gift, and those eyes,
That meete no object so base as their Master,   130
Had bin, long since, torne from that guiltie head,
And thou thy selfe slave to some needy Swisse,
Had I not worne a sword, and us'd it better
Then in thy prayers thou ere didst thy tongue.

NOVALL SENIOR.   Shall such an Insolence passe unpunisht?   135

CHARMI.   Heare mee.

ROMONT.   Yet I, that in my service done my Country,
Disdaine to bee put in the scale with thee,
Confesse my selfe unworthy to bee valued
With the least part, nay haire of the dead Marshall,   140
Of whose so many glorious undertakings,
Make choice of any one, and that the meanest
Performd against the subtill Fox of France,
The politique *Lewis*, or the more desperate Swisse,
And 'twyll outwaygh all the good purpose,   145
Though put in act, that ever Gowneman practizd.

NOVALL SENIOR.   Away with him to prison.

ROMONT.   If that curses,
Urg'd justly, and breath'd forth so, ever fell
On those that did deserve them; let not mine   150
Be spent in vaine now, that thou from this instant
Mayest in thy feare that they will fall upon thee,
Be sensible of the plagues they shall bring with them.
And for denying of a little earth,
To cover what remaynes of our great soldyer: 155
May all your wives prove whores, your factors theeves,
And while you live, your ryotous heires undoe you.
And thou, the patron of their cruelty,
Of all thy Lordships live not to be owner

F.D.—2

Of so much dung as will conceale a Dog,   160
Or what is worse, thy selfe in. And thy yeeres,
To th'end thou mayst be wretched, I wish many,
And as thou hast denied the dead a grave,
May misery in thy life make thee desire one,
Which men and all the Elements keepe from thee: 165
I have begun well, imitate, exceed.
ROCHFORT.   Good counsayle, were it a prayse worthy deed.

Exeunt OFFICERS *with* ROMONT.

DU CROYE.   Remember what we are.
CHARALOIS.   Thus low my duty
Answeres your Lordships counsaile. I will use   170
In the few words (with which I am to trouble
Your Lordships eares) the temper that you wish mee,
Not that I feare to speake my thoughts as lowd,
And with a liberty beyond *Romont*:
But that I know, for me that am made up   175
Of all that's wretched, so to haste my end,
Would seeme to most, rather a willingnesse
To quit the burthen of a hopelesse life,
Then scorne of death, or duty to the dead.
I therefore bring the tribute of my prayse   180
To your severitie, and commend the Justice,
That will not for the many services
That any man hath done the Common wealth,
Winke at his least of ills: what though my father
Writ man before he was so, and confirmd it,   185
By numbring that day, no part of his life,
In which he did not service to his Country;
Was he to be free therefore from the Lawes,
And ceremonious forme in your decrees?
Or else because he did as much as man   190
In those three memorable overthrowes
At *Granson, Morat, Nancy*, where his Master,
The warlike *Charloyes* (with whose misfortunes
I beare his name) lost treasure, men and life,
To be excus'd, from payment of those summes   195

Which (his owne patri mony spent) his zeale,
To serve his Countrey, forc'd him to take up?
NOVALL SENIOR.   The president were ill.
CHARALOIS.   And yet, my Lord, this much
  I know youll grant; After those great defeatures,   200
  Which in their dreadfull ruines buried quick,

Enter OFFICERS.

  Courage and hope, in all men but himselfe,
  He forst the proud foe, in his height of conquest,
  To yeeld unto an honourable peace.
  And in it saved an hundred thousand lives,   205
  To end his owne, that was sure proofe against
  The scalding Summers heate, and Winters frost,
  Illayres, the Cannon, and the enemies sword,
  In a most loathsome prison.
DU CROYE.   Twas his fault to be so prodigall.   210
NOVALL SENIOR.   He had from the state sufficient entertain-
ment for the Army.
CHARALOIS.   Sufficent? My Lord, you sit at home,
  And though your fees are boundlesse at the barre:
  Are thriftie in the charges of the warre.
  But your wills be obeyd. To these I turne,   215
  To these soft-hearted men, that wisely know
  They are onely good men, that pay what they owe.
FIRST CREDITOR.   And so they are.
SECOND CREDITOR.   'Tis the City Doctrine,
  We stand bound to maintaine it.   220
CHARALOIS.   Be constant in it,
  And since you are as mercilesse in your natures,
  As base, and mercenary in your meanes
  By which you get your wealth, I will not urge
  The Court to take away one scruple from   225
  The right of their lawes, or one good thought
  In you to mend your disposition with.
  I know there is no musique to your eares
  So pleasing as the groanes of men in prison,
  And that the teares of widows, and the cries   230
  Of famish'd Orphants, are the feasts that take you.

That to be in your danger, with more care
Should be avoyded, then infectious ayre,
The loath'd embraces of diseased women,
A flatterers poyson, or the losse of honour.   235
Yet rather then my fathers reverent dust
Shall want a place in that faire monument,
In which our noble Ancestors lye intomb'd,
Before the Court I offer up my selfe
A prisoner for it: loade me with those yrons   240
That have worne out his life, in my best strength
Ile run to th'incounter of cold hunger,
And choose my dwelling where no Sun dares enter,
So he may be releas'd.
FIRST CREDITOR.   What meane you sir?   245
SECOND ADVOCATE.   Onely your fee againe: ther's so much
sayd
Already in this cause, and sayd so well,
That should I onely offer to speake in it,
I should not bee heard, or laught at for it.
FIRST CREDITOR.   'Tis the first mony advocate ere gave back,   250
Though hee sayd nothing.
ROCHFORT.   Be advis'd, young Lord,
And well considerate, you throw away
Your liberty, and joyes of life together:
Your bounty is imployd upon a subject   255
That is not sensible of it, with which, wise man
Never abus'd his goodness; the great vertues
Of your dead father vindicate themselves,
From these mens malice, and breake ope the prison,
Though it containe his body.   260
NOVALL SENIOR.   Let him alone,
If he love bonds, a Gods name let him weare'em,
Provided these consent.
CHARALOIS.   I hope they are not
So ignorant in any way of profit,   265
As to neglect a possibility
To get their owne, by seeking it from that

I. II. 262 bonds] Lords Q. Previous edd. have suggested "Cords", but "bonds"
is palaeographically more likely.

Which can returne them nothing, but ill fame,
And curses for their barbarous cruelties.
THIRD CREDITOR.   What thinke you of the offer?   270
SECOND CREDITOR.   Very well.
FIRST CREDITOR.   Accept it by all meanes: let's shut him up,
   He is well-shaped and has a villanous tongue,
   And should he study that way of revenge,
   As I dare almost sweare he loves a wench,   275
   We have no wives, nor never shall get daughters
   That will hold out against him.
DU CROYE.   What's your answer?
SECOND CREDITOR.   Speake you for all.
FIRST CREDITOR.   Why, let our executions   280
   That lye upon the father, bee return'd
   Upon the sonne, and we release the body.
NOVALL SENIOR.   The Court must grant you that.
CHARALOIS.   I thanke your Lordships,
   They have in it confirm'd on me such glory,   285
   As no time can take from me: I am ready,
   Come lead me where you please: captivity
   That comes with honour, is true liberty.

                Exit CHARALOIS, CREDITORS *and* OFFICERS.

NOVALL SENIOR.   Strange rashnesse.
ROCHFORT.   A brave resolution rather,   290
   Worthy a better fortune, but however
   It is not now to be disputed, therefore
   To my owne cause. Already I have found
   Your Lordships bountifull in your favours to me,
   And that should teach my modesty to end heere   295
   And presse your loves no further.
DU CROYE.   There is nothing
   The Court can grant, but with assurance you
   May aske it, and obtaine it.
ROCHFORT.   You incourage a bold Petitioner, and 'tis not fit 300
   Your favours should be lost. Besides, 'tas beene
   A custome many yeeres, at the surrendring
   The place I now give up, to grant the President
           288 S.D. CHARALOIS] *Charmi* Q.

One boone, that parted with it. And to confirme
Your grace towards me, against all such as may   305
Detract my actions, and life hereafter,
I now preferre it to you.
DU CROYE.   Speake it freely.
ROCHFORT.   I then desire the liberty of *Romont*,
And that my Lord *Novall*, whose private wrong   310
Was equall to the injurie that was done
To the dignity of the Court, will pardon it,
And now signe his enlargement.
NOVALL SENIOR.   Pray you demand
The moyety of my estate, or any thing   315
Within my power, but this.
ROCHFORT.   Am I denyed then—my first and last request?
DU CROYE.   It must not be.
SECOND PRESIDENT.   I have a voyce to give in it.
THIRD PRESIDENT.   And I.   320
And if perswasion will not worke him to it,
We will make knowne our power.
NOVALL SENIOR.   You are too violent,
You shall have my consent—But would you had
Made tryall of my love in any thing   325
But this, you should have found then—But it skills not
You have what you desire.
ROCHFORT.   I thanke your Lordships.
DU CROYE.   The court is up, make way.

Exeunt omnes, præter ROCHFORT *and* BEAUMONT.

ROCHFORT.   I follow you—*Baumont*.   330
BEAUMONT.   My Lord.
ROCHFORT.   You are a scholler, *Baumont*,
And can search deeper into th'intents of men,
Then those that are lesse knowing—How appear'd
The piety and brave behaviour of   335
Young *Charloyes* to you?
BEAUMONT.   It is my wonder,
Since I want language to expresse it fully;
And sure the Collonell—
ROCHFORT.   Fie! he was faulty—what present mony have I?   340

BEAUMONT.   There is no want
  Of any summe a private man has use for.
ROCHFORT.   'Tis well:
  I am strangely taken with this *Charaloyes*;
  Methinks, from his example, the whole age   345
  Should learne to be good, and continue so.
  Vertue workes strangely with us: and his goodnesse
  Rising above his fortune, seems to me
  Princelike, to will, not aske a courtesie.

                                       Exeunt.

ACT II

SCENE I

Enter PONTALIER, MALOTIN, BEAUMONT.

MALOTIN.   Tis strange.
BEAUMONT.   Me thinkes so,
PONTALIER.   In a man, but young,
  Yet old in judgement, theorique, and practicke,
  In all humanity (and to increase the wonder)   5
  Religious, yet a Souldier, that he should
  Yeeld his free-living youth a captive, for
  The freedome of his aged fathers Corpes,
  And rather choose to want lifes necessaries,
  Liberty, hope of fortune, then it should   10
  In death be kept from Christian ceremony.
MALOTIN.   Come, 'Tis a golden president in a Sonne,
  To let strong nature have the better hand,
  (In such a case) of all affected reason.
  What yeeres sits on this Charolois?   15
BEAUMONT.   Twenty eight, for since the clocke did strike him 17
  old
  Under his fathers wing, this Sonne hath fought,
  Serv'd and commanded, and so aptly both,
  That sometimes he appear'd his fathers father,
  And never lesse then's sonne; the old mans vertues   20
  So recent in him, as the world may sweare,
  Nought but a faire tree, could such fayre fruit beare.

PONTALIER.   But wherefore lets he such a barbarous law,
    And men more barbarous to execute it,
    Prevaile on his soft disposition,   25
    That he had rather dye alive for debt
    Of the old man in prison, then he should
    Rob him of Sepulture, considering
    These monies borrow'd bought the lenders peace,
    And all their meanes they injoy, nor was diffus'd   30
    In any impious or licencious path?
BEAUMONT.   True: for my part, were it my fathers trunke,
    The Tyrannous Ram-heads, with their hornes should gore it,
    Or, cast it to their curres (than they) lesse currish,
    Ere prey on me so, with their Lion-law,   35
    Being in my free will (as in his) to shun it.
PONTALIER.   Alasse! he knowes himselfe (in poverty) lost:
    For in this parciall avaricious age
    What price beares Honor? Vertue? Long agoe
    It was but prays'd, and freez'd, but now a dayes   40
    'Tis colder far, and has, nor love, nor praise,
    Very prayse now freezeth too: for nature
    Did make the heathen, far more Christian then,
    Then knowledge us (lesse heathenish) Christian.
MALOTIN.   This morning is the funerall.   45
PONTALIER.   Certainely!
    And from this prison 'twas the sonnes request
    That his deare father might interment have.

                                                    Recorders
                                                    Musique.

    See, the young sonne interd a lively grave.
BEAUMONT.   They come, observe their order.   50

Enter Funerall. Body borne by four Captaines and Souldiers.
Mourners, Scutchions, etc., very good order. CHARALOIS
and ROMONT *meet it.* CHARALOIS *speaks,* ROMONT
weeping. Solemne Musique, three CREDITORS⟨, PRIEST,*
                        JAYLOR⟩.

CHARALOIS.   How like a silent streame shaded with night,
    And gliding softly with our windy sighes;

Moves the whole frame of this solemnity!
Teares, sighes and blackes, filling the simily,
Whilst I the onely murmur in this grove   55
Of death, thus hollow break forth! Vouchsafe
To stay a while, rest, rest in peace, deare earth,
Thou that brought'st rest to their unthankfull lyves,
Whose cruelty deny'd thee rest in death:
Heere stands thy poore Executor thy sonne,   60
That makes his life prisoner, to bale thy death;
Who gladlier puts on this captivity,
Then Virgins long in love, their wedding weeds:
Of all that ever thou hast done good to,
These onely have good memories, for they   65
Remember best, forget not gratitude.
I thanke you for this last and friendly love.
And tho this Country, like a viperous mother,
Not onely hath eate up ungratefully
All meanes of thee her sonne, but last thy selfe,   70
Leaving thy heire so bare and indigent,
He cannot rayse thee a poore Monument,
Such as a flatterer, or a usurer hath.
Thy worth, in every honest brest buyldes one,
Making their friendly hearts thy funerall stone.   75
PONTALIER.   Sir.
CHARALOIS.   Peace, O peace, this sceane is wholy mine.
  What weepe ye, souldiers? Blanch not, *Romont* weepes.
  Ha, let me see, my miracle is eas'd,
  The jaylors and the creditors do weepe;   80
  Even they that make us weepe, do weepe themselves.
  Be these thy bodies balme: these and thy vertue
  Keepe thy fame ever odoriferous,
  Whilst the great, proud, rich, undeserving man,
  Alive stinkes in his vices, and being vanish'd,   85
  The golden calfe that was an Idoll dect
  With Marble pillars Jet, and Porphyrie,
  Shall quickly both in bone and name consume,
  Though wrapt in lead, spice, Searecloth and perfume.
FIRST CREDITOR.   Sir.   90
CHARALOIS.   What! Away for shame: you prophane rogues

F.D.—2*

Must not be mingled with these holy reliques:
This is a Sacrifice, our showre shall crowne
His sepulcher with Olive, Myrrh and Bayes
The plants of peace, of sorrow, victorie,   95
Your teares would spring but weedes.

FIRST CREDITOR.   Would they not so?
Wee'll keepe them to stop bottles then:

ROMONT.   No; keepe'em for your owne sins, you Rogues,
Till you repent: you'll dye else and be damn'd.   100

SECOND CREDITOR.   Damn'd, ha! ha, ha.

ROMONT.   Laugh yee?

THIRD CREDITOR.   Yes faith. Sir, weel'd be very glad
To please you eyther way.

FIRST CREDITOR.   Y'are ne're content,   105
Crying nor laughing.

ROMONT.   Both with a birth yee rogues.

SECOND CREDITOR.   Our wives, Sir, taught us.

ROMONT.   Looke, looke you slaves, your thanklesse cruelty
And savage manners, of unkind *Dijon*,   110
Exhaust these flouds, and not his fathers death.

FIRST CREDITOR.   Slid, Sir, what would yee, ye'are so chole-
ricke?

SECOND CREDITOR.   Most souldiers are so yfaith, let him alone:
They have little else to live on, we have not had
A penny of him, have wee?   115

THIRD CREDITOR.   'Slight, wo'd you have our hearts?

FIRST CREDITOR.   We have nothing but his body heere in
durance
For all our mony.

PRIEST.   On.

CHARALOIS.   One moment more,   120
But to bestow a few poore legacyes,
All I have left in my dead fathers rights,
And I have done. Captaine, weare thou these spurs
That yet ne're made his horse runne from a foe.
Lieutenant, thou, this Scarfe, and may it tye   125
Thy valor, and thy honestie together:
For so it did in him. Ensigne, this Curace
Your Generalls necklace once. You gentle Bearers,

Devide this purse of gold, this other, strow
Among the poore: tis all I have. *Romont*,   130
(Weare thou this medall of himselfe) that like
A hearty Oake, grew'st close to this tall Pine,
Even in the wildest wildernesse of war,
Whereon foes broke their swords, and tyr'd themselves;
Wounded and hack'd yee were, but never fell'd.   135
For me, my portion provide in Heaven:
My roote is earth'd, and I a desolate branch
Left scattered in the high way of the world,
Trod under foot, that might have bin a Columne,
Mainely supporting our demolish'd house,   140
This would I weare as my inheritance.
And what hope can arise to me from it,
When I and it are both heere prisoners?
Onely may this, if ever we be free,
Keepe, or redeeme me from all infamie.   145

                              Song. Musicke.
                    First Song.

    Fie, cease to wonder,
    Though you heare *Orpheus* with his Ivory Lute,
    Move Trees and Rockes.
    Charme Buls, Beares, and men more savage to be mute,
    Weake foolish singer, here is one,   150
    Would have transform'd thy selfe, to stone.

FIRST CREDITOR. No farther, looke to 'em at your owne
    perill.
SECOND CREDITOR. No, as they please: their Master's a good
    man.
    I would they were i'the *Burmudas*.
JAYLOR. You must no further.   155
    The prison limits you, and the Creditors
    Exact the strictnesse.
ROMONT. Out you woolvish mungrells!
    Whose braynes should be knockt out, like dogs in July,

II. I. 145 S.D. This is the first of the four songs, which are printed separately (fol.
A2) from the text. Lockert says the songs are printed as an Appendix at the end of
the play.

Lest your infection poyson a whole towne. 160

CHARALOIS. They grudge our sorrow: your ill wills perforce
Turnes now to Charity: they would not have us
Walke too farre mourning, usurers reliefe
Grieves, if the Debtors have too much of griefe.

Exuent.

⟨SCENE II⟩

Enter BEAUMELLE: FLORIMELL: BELLAPERT.

BEAUMELLE. I prithee tell me, *Florimell*, why do women marry?

FLORIMELL. Why truly Madam, I thinke, to lye with their husbands.

BELLAPERT. You are a foole; She lyes, Madam, women marry husbands, to lye with other men. 5

FLORIMELL. Faith, eene such a woman wilt thou make. By this light, Madam, this wagtaile will spoyle you, if you take delight in her licence.

BEAUMELLE. Tis true, *Florimell*: and thou wilt make me too good for a yong Lady. What an electuary found my father out 10 for his daughter, when hee compounded you two my women! for thou, *Florimell*, art eene a graine too heavy, simply for a wayting Gentlewoman.

FLORIMELL. And thou, *Bellapert*, a graine too light.

BELLAPERT. Well, go thy wayes goodly wisdom, whom no 15 body regards. I wonder, whether be elder thou or thy hood: you thinke, because you served my Ladyes mother, are 32 yeeres old which is a peepe out, you know.

FLORIMELL. Well sayd, wherligig.

BELLAPERT. You are deceyv'd: I want a peg ith' middle. Out 20 of these Prerogatives! you thinke to be mother of the maydes heere, and mortifie em with proverbs: goe, goe, govern the sweet meates, and waigh the Suger, that the wenches steale none: say your prayers twice a day, and as I take it, you have performd your function. 25

FLORIMELL. I may bee even with you.

BELLAPERT. Harke, the Court's broke up. Goe helpe my old Lord out of his Caroch, and scratch his head till dinner time.

FLORIMELL.   Well.

Exit ⟨FLORIMELL⟩.

BELLAPERT.   Fy Madam, how you walke! By my mayden-   30
head you looke 7 yeeres older then you did this morning: why,
there can be nothing under the Sunne valuable, to make you
thus a minute.

BEAUMELLE.   Ah my sweete *Bellapert* thou Cabinet
To all my counsels, thou dost know the cause   35
That makes thy Lady wither thus in youth.

BELLAPERT.   Ud's-light, enjoy your wishes: whilst I live,
One way or other you shall crowne your will.
Would you have him your husband that you love,
And can't not bee? he is your servant though,   40
And may performe the office of a husband.

BEAUMELLE.   But there is honor, wench.

BELLAPERT.   Such a disease
There is in deed, for which ere I would dy.—

BEAUMELLE.   Prethee, distinguish me a mayd and wife.   45

BELLAPERT.   Faith, Madam, one may beare any mans children,
Tother must beare no mans.

BEAUMELLE.   What is a husband?

BELLAPERT.   Physicke, that tumbling in your belly, will make
you sicke ith'stomacke: the onely distinction betwixt a husband   50
and a servant is: the first will lye with you, when hee please;
the last shall lye with you when you please. Pray tell me, Lady,
do you love, to marry after, or would you marry, to love
after?

BEAUMELLE.   I would meete love and marriage both at once.   55

BELLAPERT.   Why then you are out of the fashion, and wilbe
contemn'd: for (Ile assure you) there are few women i'th
world, but either they have married first, and love after, or
love first, and marryed after: you must do as you may, not as
you would: your fathers will is the Goale you must fly to: 60
if a husband approch you, you would have further off, is he
you love the lesse neere you? A husband in these dayes is but
a cloake to bee oftner layde upon your bed, then in your
bed.

BEAUMELLE. Humpe.   65

BELLAPERT. Sometimes you may weare him on your shoulder, now and then under your arme: but seldome or never let him cover you: for 'tis not the fashion.

Enter YOUNG NOVALL, PONTALIER, MALOTIN, LILADAM. AYMER.

YOUNG NOVALL. Best day to natures curiosity,
Starre of *Dijum*, the lustre of all *France*,   70
Perpetuall spring dwell on thy rosy cheekes,
Whose breath is perfume to our Continent,
See *Flora* turn'd in her varieties.

BELLAPERT. Oh divine Lord!

YOUNG NOVALL. No autumne, nor no age ever approach   75
This heavenly piece, which nature having wrought,
She lost her needle and did then despaire,
Ever to worke so lively and so faire.

LILADAM. Uds light, my Lord, one of the purles of your band is (without all discipline) falne out of his ranke.   80

YOUNG NOVALL. How? I would not for a 1000 crownes she had seen't.
Deare *Liladam*, reforme it.

BELLAPERT. Oh Lord: *Per se*, Lord, quintessence of honour, shee walkes not under a weede that could deny thee any thing. 85

BEAUMELLE. Prethy peace, wench, thou dost but blow the fire, that flames too much already.

Liladam ⟨and⟩ *Aymer trim Novall,*
            whilst Bellapert ⟨attends to⟩ *her Lady.*

AYMER. By gad, my Lord, you have the divinest Taylor of Christendome; he hath made you looke like an Angell in your cloth of Tissue doublet.   90

PONTALIER. This is a three-leg'd Lord, ther's a fresh assault, oh that men should spend time thus!
See see, how her blood drives to her heart, and straight vaults to her cheekes againe.

MALOTIN. What are these?   95

PONTALIER. One of 'em there the lower is a good, foolish, knavish, sociable gallimaufry of a man, and has much taught

my Lord with singing, hee is master of a musicke house: the
other is his dressing blocke, upon whom my Lord layes all
his cloathes, and fashions, ere he vouchsafes 'em his owne 100
person; you shall see him i'th morning in the Gally-slops, at
noone in the Bullion, i'th evening in Quirpo, and all night
in—

MALOTIN.   A Bawdyhouse.

PONTALIER.   If my Lord deny, they deny, if hee affirme, they 105
affirme: they skip into my Lords cast skins some twice a yeere,
and thus they lie to eate, eate to live, and live to prayse my
Lord.

MALOTIN.   Good sir, tell me one thing.

PONTALIER.   What's that?   110

MALOTIN.   Dare these men ever fight, on any cause?

PONTALIER.   Oh no, 'twould spoyle their cloathes, and put their
bands out of order.

YOUNG NOVALL.   Mistress, you heare the news: your father has
resign'd his Presidentship to my Lord my father.   115

MALOTIN.   And Lord *Charolois* undone forever.

PONTALIER.   Troth, 'tis pity, sir.
A braver hope of so assur'd a father
Did never comfort *France*.

LILADAM.   A good dumbe mourner.   120

AYMER.   A silent blacke.

YOUNG NOVALL.   Oh fie upon him, how he weares his cloathes!
As if he had come this Christmas from St. *Omers*,
To see his friends, and return'd after Twelfetyde.

LILADAM.   His Colonell lookes fienely like a drover.   125

YOUNG NOVALL.   That had a winter ly'n perdieu i'th rayne.

AYMER.   What, he that weares a clout about his necke,
His cuffes in's pocket, and his heart in's mouth?

YOUNG NOVALL.   Now out upon him!

BEAUMELLE.   Servant, tye my hand.   130
How your lips blush, in scorne that they should pay
Tribute to hands, when lips are in the way!

YOUNG NOVALL.   I thus recant, yet now your hand looks white,
Because your lips robd it of such a right.

Monsieur Aymour, I prethy sing the song   135
Devoted to my Mistress.

                                          Cant⟨at⟩.   *Musicke.*

⟨AYMER *sings.*⟩

                           Second Song.

Man.

Set *Phoebus*, set, a fayrer sunne doth rise,
From the bright Radience of my Mistress' eyes
Then ever thou begat'st. I dare not looke,
Each haire a golden line, each word a hooke,   140
The more I strive, the more still I am tooke.

Wom.

Fayre servant, come, the day these eyes doe lend
To warme thy blood, thou dost so vainely spend.
Come strangle breath.

Man.

What noate so sweet as this,   145
That calles the spirits to a further blisse?

Wom.

Yet this out-savours wine, and this Perfume.

Man.

Let's die, I languish, I consume.

After the Song, Enter ROCHFORT, *and* BEAUMONT.

BEAUMONT.   *Romont* will come, sir, straight.
ROCHFORT.   'Tis well.   150
BEAUMELLE.   My Father.
YOUNG NOVALL.   My honorable Lord.
ROCHFORT.   My Lord *Novall*, this is a vertue in you,
   So early up and ready before noone,
   That are the map of dressing through all *France*.   155
YOUNG NOVALL.   I rise to say my prayers, sir, heere's my Saint.
ROCHFORT.   Tis well and courtly: you must give me leave,
   I have some private conference with my daughter,
   Pray use my garden, you shall dine with me.
LILADAM.   Wee'l waite on you.   160

    136–48 This song is headed in Q "Second Song. II A Dialogue between *Nouall*,
and *Beaumelle.*" In Q the lining of this song is wrong and it is given here re-
aligned to fit the rhyme-scheme.

YOUNG NOVALL. Good morne unto your Lordship,
Remember what you have vow'd—

⟨*Aside*,⟩ *to* BEAUMELLE.

BEAUMELLE. Performe I must.

Exeunt omnes, præter ROCHFORT, BEAUMELLE.

ROCHFORT. Why how now *Beaumelle*, thou look'st not well,
Th'art sad of late, come cheere thee, I have found   165
A wholesome remedy for these mayden fits,
A goodly Oake whereon to twist my vine,
Till her faire branches grow up to the starres.
Be neere at hand, successe crowne my intent,
My businesse fills my little time so full,   170
I cannot stand to talke: I know, thy duty
Is handmayd to my will, especially
When it presents nothing but good and fit.
BEAUMELLE. Sir, I am yours. Oh if my feares prove true,
Fate hath wrong'd love, and will destroy me too.   175

Exit BEAUMELLE.

Enter ROMONT, KEEPER.

ROMONT. Sent you for me, sir?
ROCHFORT. Yes.
ROMONT. Your Lordships pleasure?
ROCHFORT. Keeper, this prisoner I will see forthcomming
Upon my word—Sit downe good Colonell.   180

Exit KEEPER.

Why I did wish you hither, noble sir,
Is to advise you from this yron carriage,
Which, so affected, *Romont*, you weare,
To pity and to counsell yee submit
With expedition to the great *Novall*:   185
Recant your sterne contempt, and slight neglect
Of the whole Court, and him, and opportunity,
Or you will undergoe a heavy censure
In publique very shortly.
ROMONT. Hum hum: reverend sir,   190
I have observ'd you, and doe know you well,

And am now more affraid you know not me,
By wishing my submission to *Novall*,
Then I can be of all the bellowing mouthes
That waite upon him to pronounce the censure,   195
Could it determine me torments, and shame.
Submit, and crave forgivenesse of a beast?
Tis true, this bile of state weares purple Tissue,
Is fed high, proud: so is his Lordships horse,
And beares as rich Caparisons. I know,   200
This Elephant carries on his backe not onely
Towres, Castles, but the ponderous republique,
And never stoops for't, with his strong-breath'd trunk
Snuffes others titles, Lordships, Offices,
Wealth, bribes, and lyves, under his ravenous jawes.   205
Whats this unto my freedome? I dare dye;
And therfore aske this Cammell, if these blessings
(For so they would be understood by a man)
But mollifie one rudenesse in his nature,
Sweeten the eager relish of the law,   210
At whose great helme he sits: helps he the poore
In a just businesse? nay, does he not crosse
Every deserved souldier and scholler,
As if when nature made him, she had made
The generall Antipathy of all vertue?   215
How savagely, and blasphemously hee spake
Touching the Generall, the grave Generall dead,
I must weepe when I thinke on't.
ROCHFORT.   Sir.
ROMONT.   My Lord, I am not stubborne, I can melt, you see,   220
And prize a vertue better then my life:
For though I be not learned, I ever lov'd
That holy Mother of all issues, good,
Whose white hand (for a Scepter) holdes a File
To pollish roughest customes, and in you   225
She has her right: see, I am calme as sleepe,
But when I thinke of the gross injuries,
The godlesse wrong done, to my Generall dead,
I rave indeed, and could eate this *Novall*
A soul-lesse Dromodary.   230

ROCHFORT.   Oh bee temperate,
  Sir, though I would perswade, I'le not constraine:
  Each mans opinion freely is his owne,
  Concerning any thing or any body,
  Be it right or wrong, tis at the Judges perill.   235

Enter BEAUMONT.

BEAUMONT.   These men, Sir, waite without, my Lord is come too.
ROCHFORT.   Pay'em those summes upon the table, take
  Their full releases: stay, I want a witnesse:
  Let mee intreat you Colonell, to walke in,
  And stand but by, to see this money pay'd,   240
  It does concerne you and your friends, it was
  The better cause you were sent for, though sayd otherwise.
  The deed shall make this my request more plaine.
ROMONT.   I shall obey your pleasure Sir, though ignorant
  To what it tends.   245

                    Exit BEAUMONT: ROMONT.
Enter CHARALOIS.

ROCHFORT.   Worthiest Sir,
  You are most welcome: fye, no more of this:
  You have out-wept a woman, noble *Charolois*.
  No man but has, or must bury a father.
CHARALOIS.   Grave Sir, I buried sorrow, for his death,   250
  In the grave with him. I did never thinke
  Hee was immortall, though I vow I grieve,
  And see no reason why the vicious,
  Vertuous, valiant and unworthy men
  Should dye alike.   255
ROCHFORT.   They do not.
CHARALOIS.   In the manner
  Of dying, Sir, they do not, but all dye,
  And therein differ not: but I have done.
  I spy'd the lively picture of my father,   260
  Passing your gallery, and that cast this water
  Into mine eyes: see, foolish that I am,
  To let it doe so.
ROCHFORT.   Sweete and gentle nature,

How silken is this well comparatively   265
To other men! I have a suite to you Sir.
CHARALOIS.   Take it, tis granted.
ROCHFORT.   What?
CHARALOIS.   Nothing, my Lord.
ROCHFORT.   Nothing is quickly granted.   270
CHARALOIS.   Faith, my Lord,
   That nothing granted, is even all I have,
   For (all know) I have nothing left to grant.
ROCHFORT.   Sir, ha' you any suite to me? Ill grant
You some thing, any thing.   275
CHARALOIS.   Nay surely, I that can
   Give nothing, will but sue for that againe.
   No man will grant mee any thing I sue for.
   But begging nothing, every man will give't.
ROCHFORT.   Sir, the love I bore your father, and the worth   280
   I see in you, so much resembling his,
   Made me thus send for you. And tender heere

                                        Drawes a Curtayne.

What ever you will take, gold, Jewels, both,
All, to supply your wants, and free your selfe.
Where heavenly vertue in high blouded veines   285
Is lodg'd, and can agree, men should kneele downe,
Adore, and sacrifice all that they have;
And well they may, it is so seldome seene.
Put off your wonder, and heere freely take
Or send your servants. Nor, Sir, shall you use   290
In ought of this, a poore mans fee, or bribe,
Unjustly taken of the rich, but what's
Directly gotten, and yet by the Law.
CHARALOIS.   How ill, Sir, it becomes those haires to mocke!
ROCHFORT.   Mocke? thunder strike mee then.   295
CHARALOIS.   You doe amaze mee:
   But you shall wonder too, I will not take
   One single piece of this great heape: why should I
   Borrow, that have not meanes to pay, nay am
   A very bankerupt, even in flattering hope   300

Of ever raysing any. All my begging,
Is *Romonts* libertie.

Enter ROMONT, CREDITORS *loaden with mony*, BEAUMONT.

ROCHFORT.   Heere is your friend,
Enfranchist ere you spake. I give him you,
And *Charolois*, I give you to your friend   305
As free a man as hee; your fathers debts
Are taken off.

CHARALOIS.   How?

ROMONT.   Sir, it is most true.
I am the witnes.   310

FIRST CREDITOR.   Yes faith, wee are pay'd.

SECOND CREDITOR.   Heaven blesse his Lordship, I did thinke
him wiser.

THIRD CREDITOR.   He a states-man, he an asse. Pay other mens
debts?   315

FIRST CREDITOR.   That hee was never bound for.

ROMONT.   One more such would save the rest of pleaders.

CHARALOIS.   Honord *Rochfort*.
Lye still my toung and blushes scald my cheekes,
That offer thankes in words, for such great deeds.   320

ROCHFORT.   Call in my daughter: still I have a suit to you,
Would you requite mee.

                                        Exit BEAUMONT.

ROMONT.   With his life, assure you.

ROCHFORT.   Nay, would you make me now your debter, Sir.

Enter BEAUMONT, BEAUMELLE.

This is my onely child: what shee appeares   325
Your Lordship well may see, her education
Followes not any: for her mind, I know it
To be far fayrer then her shape, and hope
It will continue so: if now her birth
Be not too meane for *Charolois*, take her   330
This virgin by the hand, and call her wife,
Indowd with all my fortunes: blesse mee so,
Requite thee thus, and make mee happier,
In joyning my poore empty name to yours,
Then if my state were multiplied ten fold.   335

CHARALOIS.   Is this the payment, Sir, that you expect?
  Why, you participate me more in debt,
  That nothing but my life can ever pay,
  This beautie being your daughter, in which yours
  I must conceive necessitie of her vertue,   340
  Without all dowry is a Princes ayme,
  Then, as shee is, for poore and worthlesse I,
  How much too worthy! Waken me, *Romont*,
  That I may know I dream't, and find this vanisht.
ROMONT.   Sure, I sleepe not.   345
ROCHFORT.   Your sentence life or death.
CHARALOIS.   Faire *Beaumelle*, can you love me?
BEAUMELLE.   Yes, my Lord.

Enter YOUNG NOVALL, PONTALIER, MALOTIN, LILADAM.
AYMER. *All salute.*

CHARALOIS.   You need not question me, if I can you.
  You are the fayrest virgin in *Digum*,   350
  And *Rochfort* is your father.
YOUNG NOVALL.   What's this change?
ROCHFORT.   You met my wishes, Gentlemen.
  ROMONT.   What make
  These dogs in doublets heere?   355
BEAUMONT.   A Visitation, Sir.
CHARALOIS.   Then thus, Faire *Beaumelle*, I write my faith
  Thus seale it in the sight of Heaven and men.
  Your fingers tye my heart-strings with this touch
  In true-love knots, which nought but death shall loose.   360
  And let these teares (an Embleme of our loves)
  Like Cristall rivers individually
  Flow into one another, make one source,
  Which never man distinguish, lesse devide:
  Breath, marry, breath, and kisses, mingle soules.   365
  Two hearts, and bodies, heere incorporate:
  And though with little wooing I have wonne,
  My future life shall bee a wooing tyme.
  And every day, new as the bridall one.
  Oh Sir, I groane under your courtesies,   370

      361 let these teares] yet these eares Q.

More then my fathers bones under his wrongs,
You *Curtius*-like, have throwne into the gulfe,
Of this his Countries foule ingratitude,
Your life and fortunes, to redeeme their shames.

ROCHFORT.   No more, my glory, come, let's in and hasten   375
This celebration.

ROMONT. MALOTIN. PONTALIER. BEAUMONT.
All faire blisse upon it.

Exeunt ROCHFORT, CHARALOIS, ROMONT, BEAUMONT,
                                        MALOTIN.

YOUNG NOVALL.   Mistresse.

BEAUMELLE.   Oh servant, vertue strengthen me.
Thy presence blowes round my affections vane: 380
You will undoe me, if you speake againe.

Exit BEAUMELLE.

LILADAM.   *Aymer*, here will be sport for you. This workes.

Exeunt LILADAM, AYMER.

YOUNG NOVALL.   Peace, peace.

PONTALIER.   One word, my Lord *Novall.*

YOUNG NOVALL.   What, thou wouldst mony; there.   385

PONTALIER.   No, Ile none, Ile not be bought a slave,
A Pander, or a Parasite, for all
Your fathers worth, though you have sav'd my life,
Rescued me often from my wants, I must not
Winke at your follyes: that will ruine you.   390
You know my blunt way, and my love to truth:
Forsake the pursuit of this Ladies honour,
Now you doe see her made another mans,
And such a mans, so good, so popular,
Or you will plucke a thousand mischiefes on you.   395
The benefits you have done me, are not lost,
Nor cast away, they are purs'd heere in my heart,
But let me pay you, sir, a fayrer way
Then to defend your vices, or to sooth'em.

YOUNG NOVALL.   Ha, ha, ha, what are my courses unto thee?   400

Good Cousin *Pontalier*, meddle with that
That shall concerne thy selfe.

Exit NOVALL.

PONTALIER.   No more but scorne?
Move on then, starres, worke your pernicious will.
Onely the wise rule, and prevent your ill.   405

Exit.
Hoboyes.

*Here a passage over the Stage, while the Act is playing for the Marriage
of Charalois with Beaumelle, etc.*

ACT III

SCENE I

Enter YOUNG NOVALL, BELLAPERT.

YOUNG NOVALL.   Flie not to these excuses: thou hast bin
False in thy promise, and when I have said
Ungratefull, all is spoke.
BELLAPERT.   Good my Lord, but heare me onely.
YOUNG NOVALL.   To what purpose, trifler?   5
Can any thing that thou canst say, make voyd
The marriage? or those pleasures but a dreame,
Which *Charaloyes* (oh *Venus*) hath enjoyed?
BELLAPERT.   I yet could say that you receive advantage,
In what you thinke a losse, would you vouchsafe me   10
That you were never in the way till now
With safety to arrive at your desires,
That pleasure makes love to you unattended
By danger of repentance?
YOUNG NOVALL.   That I could   15
But apprehend one reason how this might be,
Hope would not then forsake me.
BELLAPERT.   The enjoying
Of what you most desire, I say th'enjoying
Shall, in the full possession of your wishes,   20
Confirme that I am faithfull.

YOUNG NOVALL.   Give some rellish
How this may appeare possible.
BELLAPERT.   I will—
Rellish, and taste, and make the banquet easie: 25
You say my Ladie's married. I confesse it,
That *Charalois* hath injoyed her, 'tis most true
That with her, hee's already Master of
The best part of my old Lords state. Still better,
But that the first, or last, should be your hindrance,   30
I utterly deny: for but observe me:
While she went for, and was, I sweare, a Virgin,
What courtesie could she with her honour give
Or you receive with safety—take me with you,
When I say courtesie, doe not thinke I meane   35
A kisse, the tying of her shoo or garter,
An houre of private conference: those are trifles.
In this word courtesy, we that are gamesters point at
The sport direct, where not alone the lover
Brings his Artillery, but uses it.   40
Which word expounded to you, such a courtesie
Doe you expect, and sudden.
YOUNG NOVALL.   But he tasted the first sweetes, *Bellapert.*
BELLAPERT.   He wrong'd you shrewdly,
He toyled to climbe up to the *Phœnix* nest,   45
And in his prints leaves your ascent more easie.
I doe not know, you that are perfect Crittiques
In womens bookes, may talke of maydenheads.
YOUNG NOVALL.   But for her marriage.
BELLAPERT.   'Tis a faire protection   50
'Gainst all arrests of feare, or shame for ever.
Such as are faire, and yet not foolish, study
To have one at thirteene; but they are mad
That stay till twenty. Then sir, for the pleasure,
To say Adulterie's sweeter, that is stale.   55
This onely: is not the contentment more,
To say, This is my Cuckold, then my Rivall?
More I could say—but briefely, she doates on you,
If it prove otherwise, spare not, poyson me
With next gold you give me.   60

Enter BEAUMELLE.

BEAUMELLE.   Hows this servant, courting my woman?
BELLAPERT.   As an entrance to
    The favour of the mistris: you are together
    And I am perfect in my qu.
BEAUMELLE.   Stay *Bellapert*.   65
BELLAPERT.   In this, I must not with your leave obey you.
    Your Taylor and your Tire-woman waite without
    And stay my counsayle, and direction for
    Your next dayes dressing. I have much to doe,
    Nor will your Ladiship now, time is precious,   70
    Continue idle: this choise Lord will finde
    So fit imployment for you.

                           Exit BELLAPERT.

BEAUMELLE.   I shall grow angry.
YOUNG NOVALL.   Not so, you have a jewell in her, Madam.

Enter ⟨BELLAPERT⟩ *againe.*

BELLAPERT.   I had forgot to tell your Ladiship   75
    The closet is private and your couch ready;
    And if you please that I shall loose the key,
    But say so, and tis done.

                           Exit BELLAPERT.

BEAUMELLE.   You come to chide me, servant, and bring with you
    Sufficient warrant, you will say and truely,   80
    My father found too much obedience in me,
    By being won too soone: yet if you please
    But to remember, all my hopes and fortunes
    Had reverence to his liking: you will grant
    That though I did not well towards you, I yet   85
    Did wisely for my selfe.
YOUNG NOVALL.   With too much fervor
    I have so long lov'd and still love you, Mistresse,
    To esteeme that an injury to me
    Which was to you convenient: that is past   90
    My helpe, is past my cure. You yet may, Lady,
    In recompence of all my dutious service,

(Provided that your will answere your power)
Become my Creditresse.
BEAUMELLE.   I understand you,   95
    And for assurance, the request you make
    Shall not be long unanswered. Pray you sit,
    And by what you shall heare, you'l easily finde,
    My passions are much fitter to desire,
    Then to be sued to.   100

Enter ROMONT *and* FLORIMELL.

FLORIMELL.   Sir, tis not envy
    At the start my fellow has got of me in
    My Ladies good opinion, that's the motive
    Of this discovery; but due payment
    Of what I owe her Honour.   105
ROMONT.   So I conceive it.
FLORIMELL.   I have observ'd too much, nor shall my silence
    Prevent the remedy—yonder they are,
    I dare not bee seene with you. You may doe
    What you thinke fit, which wilbe, I presume,   110
    The office of a faithfull and tryed friend
    To my young Lord.
                                        Exit FLORIMELL.
ROMONT.   This is no vision: ha!
YOUNG NOVALL.   With the next opportunity.
BEAUMELLE.   By this kisse, and this, and this.   115
YOUNG NOVALL.   That you would ever sweare thus.
ROMONT.   If I seeme rude, your pardon, Lady; yours
    I do not aske; come, do not dare to shew mee
    A face of anger, or the least dislike.
    Put on, and suddainly a milder looke,   120
    I shall grow rough else.
YOUNG NOVALL.   What have I done, Sir,
    To draw this harsh unsavory language from you?
ROMONT.   Done, Popinjay? why, dost thou thinke that if
    I ere had dreamt that thou hadst done me wrong,   125
    Thou shouldest outlive it?
BEAUMELLE.   This is something more
    Then my Lords friendship gives commission for.

YOUNG NOVALL.   Your presence and the place, makes him
  presume
  Upon my patience.   130
ROMONT.   As if thou ere wer't angry
  But with thy Taylor, and yet that poore shred
  Can bring more to the making up of a man,
  Then can be hop'd from thee: thou art his creature,
  And did hee not each morning new create yee   135
  Thou wouldst stinke and be forgotten. Ile not change
  On sillable more with thee, untill thou bring
  Some testimony under good mens hands,
  Thou art a Christian. I suspect thee strongly,
  And wilbe satisfied: till which time, keepe from me.   140
  The entertainment of your visitation
  Has made what I intended on a businesse.
YOUNG NOVALL.   So wee shall meete—Madam.
ROMONT.   Use that legge againe, and Ile cut off the other.
YOUNG NOVALL.   Very good.   145

                                          Exit NOVALL.

ROMONT.   What a perfume the Muske-cat leaves behind him!
  Do you admit him for a property,
  To save you charges, Lady?
BEAUMELLE.   Tis not uselesse,
  Now you are to succeed him.   150
ROMONT.   So I respect you,
  Not for your selfe, but in remembrance of,
  Who is your father, and whose wife you now are,
  That I choose rather not to understand
  Your nasty scoffe then,—   155
BEAUMELLE.   What, you will not beate mee,
  If I expound it to you. Heer's a Tyrant
  Spares neyther man nor woman.
ROMONT.   My intents
  Madam, deserve not this; nor do I stay   160
  To bee the whetstone of your wit: preserve it
  To spend on such, as know how to admire
  Such coloured stuffe. In me there is now speaks to you
  As true a friend and servant to your Honour,

And one that will with as much hazzard guard it,   165
As ever man did goodnesse.—But then Lady,
You must endeavour not alone to bee,
But to appeare worthy such love and service.
BEAUMELLE.   To what tends this?
ROMONT.   Why, to this purpose, Lady,   170
I do desire you should prove such a wife
To *Charaloys* (and such a one hee merits)
As Cæsar, did hee live, could not except at,
Not onely innocent from crime, but free
From all taynt and suspition.   175
BEAUMELLE.   They are base that judge me otherwise.
ROMONT.   But yet bee carefull.
Detraction's a bold monster, and feares not
To wound the fame of Princes, if it find
But any blemish in their lives to worke on.   180
But Ile bee plainer with you: had the people
Bin learnd to speake, but what even now I saw,
Their malice out of that would raise an engine
To overthrow your honor. In my sight
(With yonder pointed foole I frighted from you)   185
You us'd familiarity beyond
A modest entertaynment: you embrac'd him
With too much ardor for a stranger, and
Met him with kisses neyther chaste nor comely:
But learne you to forget him, as I will   190
Your bounties to him, you will find it safer
Rather to bee uncourtly, then immodest.
BEAUMELLE.   This prety rag about your necke shews well,
And being coorse and little worth, it speakes you,
As terrible as thrifty.   195
ROMONT.   Madam.
BEAUMELLE.   Yes.
And this strong belt in which you hang your honor
Will out-last twenty scarfs.
ROMONT.   What meane you, Lady?   200
BEAUMELLE.   And all else about you Cap a pe,
So uniforme in spite of handsomnesse,
Shews such a bold contempt of comelinesse,

That tis not strange your Laundresse in the League,
Grew mad with love of you.   205
ROMONT.   Is my free counsayle
Answerd with this ridiculous scorne?
BEAUMELLE.   These objects
Stole very much of my attention from me,
Yet something I remember, to speake truth,   210
Delyverd gravely, but to little purpose,
That almost would have made me sweare, some Curate
Had stolne into the person of *Romont*,
And in the praise of goodwife honesty,
Had read an homely.   215
ROMONT.   By thy hand.
BEAUMELLE.   And sword,
I will make up your oath, twill want weight else.
You are angry with me, and poore I laugh at it.
Do you come from the Campe, which affords onely   220
The conversation of cast suburbe whores,
To set downe to a Lady of my ranke,
Lymits of entertainmment?
ROMONT.   Sure a Legion has possest this woman.
BEAUMELLE.   One stamp more would do well: yet I desire not   225
You should grow horne-mad, till you have a wife.
You are come to warme meate, and perhaps cleane linnen:
Feed, weare it, and bee thankfull. For me, know,
That though a thousand watches were set on mee,
And you the Master-spy, I yet would use,   230
The liberty that best likes mee. I will revell,
Feast, kisse, imbreace, perhaps grant larger favours:
Yet such as live upon my meanes, shall know
They must not murmur at it. If my Lord
Bee now growne yellow, and has chose you out   235
To serve his Jealouzy that way, tell him this,
You have something to informe him.

Exit BEAUMELLE.

ROMONT.   And I will.
Beleeve it wicked one I will. Heare, Heaven,

III. I. 211 Delyverd] Deceyued Q.

But hearing pardon mee: if these fruts grow   240
Upon the tree of marriage, let me shun it,
As a forbidden sweete. An heyre and rich,
Young, beautifull, yet adde to this a wife,
And I will rather choose a Spittle sinner
Carted an age before, though three parts rotten,   245
And take it for a blessing, rather then
Be fettered to the hellish slavery
Of such an impudence.

Enter BEAUMONT *with writings.*

BEAUMONT.   Collonell, good fortune
To meet you thus: you looke sad, but Ile tell you   250
Something that shall remove it. Oh how happy
Is my Lord *Charaloys* in his faire bride!
ROMONT.   A happy man indeede!—pray you in what?
BEAUMONT.   I dare sweare, you would thinke so good a Lady,
A dower sufficient.   255
ROMONT.   No doubt. But on.
BEAUMONT.   So faire, so chaste, so vertuous: so indeed
    All that is excellent.
ROMONT.   Women have no cunning to gull the world.
BEAUMONT.   Yet to all these, my Lord   260
Her father gives the full addition of
All he does now possesse in *Burgundy*:
These writings to confirme it, are new seal'd
And I most fortunate to present him with them,
I must goe seeke him out, can you direct mee?   265
ROMONT.   You'l finde him breaking a young horse.
BEAUMONT.   I thanke you.

                          Exit BEAUMONT.

ROMONT.   I must do something worthy *Charaloys* friendship.
If she were well inclin'd—to keepe her so,
Deserv'd not thankes: and yet to stay a woman   270
Spur'd headlong by hot lust, to her owne ruine,
Is harder then to prop a falling towre
With a deceiving reed.

Enter ROCHFORT.

ROCHFORT.   Some one seeke for me,
  As soone as he returnes.   275
ROMONT.   Her father! ha!
  How if I breake this to him? sure it cannot
  Meete with an ill construction. His wisedome
  Made powerfull by the authority of a father,
  Will warrant and give priviledge to his counsailes.   280
  It shall be so—my Lord.
ROCHFORT.   Your friend Romont: would you ought with me?
ROMONT.   I stand so ingag'd
  To your so many favours, that I hold it
  A breach in thankfulnesse, should I not discover,   285
  Though with some imputation to my selfe,
  All doubts that may concerne you.
ROCHFORT.   The performance
  Will make this protestation worth my thanks.
ROMONT.   Then with your patience lend me your attention   290
  For what I must deliver, whispered onely
  You will with too much griefe receive.

Enter BEAUMELLE, BELLAPERT.

BEAUMELLE. ⟨*Aside, to* BELLAPERT⟩   See wench!
  Upon my life as I forspake, hee's now
  Preferring his complaint: but be thou perfect,   295
  And we will fit him.
BELLAPERT.   Feare not me, pox on him:
  A Captaine turne Informer against kissing!
  Would he were hang'd up in his rusty Armour:
  But if our fresh wits cannot turne the plots   300
  Of such a mouldy murrion on it selfe;
  Rich cloathes, choyse fare, and a true friend at a call,
  With all the pleasures the night yeelds, forsake us.
ROCHFORT.   This is my daughter? doe not wrong her.
BELLAPERT.   Now begin.   305
  The games afoot, and wee in distance.
BEAUMELLE. ⟨*Aloud*⟩   Tis thy fault, foolish girle, pinne on my
    vaile,
  I will not weare those jewels. Am I not
  Already matcht beyond my hopes? yet still

You prune and set me forth, as if I were   310
Againe to please a suyter.
BELLAPERT.   Tis the course
That our great Ladies take.
ROMONT.   A weake excuse.
BEAUMELLE.   Those that are better seene, in what concernes   315
A Ladies honour and faire fame, condemne it.
You waite well, in your absence, my Lords friend
The understanding, grave and wise *Romont*—
ROMONT.   Must I be still her sport?
BEAUMELLE.   Reprov'd me for it.   320
And he has traveld to bring home a judgement
Not to be contradicted. You will say
My father, that owes more to yeeres then he,
Has brought me up to musique, language, Courtship,
And I must use them.   True, but not t'offend,   325
Or render me suspected.
ROCHFORT.   Does your fine story begin from this?
BEAUMELLE.   I thought a parting kisse
From young *Novall*, would have displeasd no more
Then heretofore it hath done; but I finde   330
I must restrayne such favours now; looke therefore   4
As you are carefull to continue mine,
That I no more be visited. Ile endure
The strictest course of life that jealousie
Can thinke secure enough, ere my behaviour   335
Shall call my fame in question.
ROMONT.   Ten dissemblers
Are in this subtile devill. You beleeve this?
ROCHFORT.   So farre that if you trouble me againe
With a report like this, I shall not onely   340
Judge you malicious in your disposition,
But study to repent what I have done
To such a nature.
ROMONT.   Why, 'tis exceeding well.
ROCHFORT.   And for you, daughter, off with this, off with it: 345

⟨Removing veil.⟩

I have that confidence in your goodnesse, I,

That I will not consent to have you live
Like to a Recluse in a cloyster: goe
Call in the gallants, let them make you merry,
Use all fit liberty.   350
BELLAPERT.   Blessing on you.
  If this new preacher with the sword and feather
  Could prove his doctrine for Canonicall,
  We should have a fine world.

                                        Exit BELLAPERT.

ROCHFORT.   Sir, if you please   355
  To beare your selfe as fits a Gentleman,
  The house is at your service: but if not,
  Though you seeke company else where, your absence
  Will not be much lamented—

                                        Exit ROCHFORT.

ROMONT.   If this be   360
  The recompence of striving to preserve
  A wanton gigglet honest, very shortly
  'Twill make all mankinde Panders—Do you smile,
  Good Lady Loosenes? your whole sex is like you,
  And that man's mad that seekes to better any: 365
  What new change have you next?
BEAUMELLE.   Oh, feare not you, sir,
  Ile shift into a thousand, but I will
  Convert your heresie.
ROMONT.   What heresie? Speake.   370
BEAUMELLE.   Of keeping a Lady that is married,
  From entertayning servants.—

Enter YOUNG NOVALL, MALOTIN, LILADAM, AYMER,
PONTALIER.

  O, you are welcome.
  Use any meanes to vexe him,
  And then with welcome follow me.   375

                                        Exit BEAUMELLE.

YOUNG NOVALL.   You are tyr'd
  With your grave exhortations, Collonell.

LILADAM.   How is it? Fayth, your Lordship may doe well,
   To helpe him to some Church-preferment: 'tis
   Now the fashion, for men of all conditions,   380
   How ever they have liv'd, to end that way.
AYMER.   That face would doe well in a surplesse.
ROMONT.   Rogues, be silent—or—
PONTALIER.   S'death will you suffer this?
ROMONT.   And you, the master Rogue, the coward rascall,   385
   I shall be with you suddenly.
YOUNG NOVALL.   *Pontallier,*
   If I should strike him, I know I shall kill him:
   And therefore I would have thee beate him, for
   Hee's good for nothing else.   390
LILADAM.   His backe
   Appeares to me, as it would tire a Beadle,
   And then he has a knotted brow, would bruise
   A courtlike hand to touch it.
AYMER.   Hee lookes like   395
   A Curryer when his hides grown deare.
PONTALIER.   Take heede he curry not some of you.
YOUNG NOVALL.   Gods me, hee's angry.
ROMONT.   I breake no Jests, but I can breake my sword
   About your pates.   400

Enter CHARALOIS *and* BEAUMONT.

LILADAM.   Heres more.
AYMER.   Come let's bee gone,
   Wee are beleaguerd.
YOUNG NOVALL.   Looke they bring up their troups.
PONTALIER.   Will you sit downe with this disgrace?   405
   You are abus'd most grosely.
LILADAM.   I grant you, Sir, we are, and you would have us
   Stay and be more abus'd.
YOUNG NOVALL.   My Lord, I am sorry,
   Your house is so inhospitable, we must quit it.   410

Exeunt. Manent CHARALOIS, ROMONT.

CHARALOIS.   Prethee *Romont,* what caus'd this uprore?

ROMONT.   Nothing.
  They laugh'd and us'd their scurvy wits upon mee.
CHARALOIS.   Come, tis thy Jealous nature: but I wonder
  That you which are an honest man and worthy,   415
  Should foster this suspition: no man laughes;
  No one can whisper, but thou apprehend'st
  His conference and his scorne reflects on thee:
  For my part they should scoffe their thin wits out,
  So I not heard 'em, beate me, not being there.   420
  Leave, leave these fits, to conscious men, to such
  As are obnoxious, to those foolish things
  As they can gibe at.
ROMONT.   Well, Sir.
CHARALOIS.   Thou art know'n   425
  Valiant without defect, right defin'd,
  Which is (as fearing to doe injury,
  As tender to endure it) not a brabbler,
  A swearer.
ROMONT.   Pish, pish, what needs this my Lord?   430
  If I bee knowne none such, how vainly, you
  Do cast away good counsaile? I have lov'd you,
  And yet must freely speake: so young a tutor,
  Fits not so old a Souldier as I am.
  And I must tell you, t'was in your behalfe   435
  I grew inraged thus, yet had rather dye,
  Then open the great cause a syllable further.
CHARALOIS.   In my behalfe? wherein hath *Charalois*
  Unfitly so demean'd himselfe, to give
  The least occasion to the loosest tongue,   440
  To throw aspersions on him, or so weakely
  Protected his owne honor, as it should
  Need a defence from any but himselfe?
  They are fooles that judge me by my outward seeming,
  Why should my gentlenesse beget abuse?   445
  The Lion is not angry that does sleepe,
  Nor every man a Coward that can weepe.
  For Gods sake speake the cause.
ROMONT.   Not for the world.
  Oh it will strike disease into your bones   450

Beyond the cure of physicke, drinke your blood,
Rob you of all your rest, contract your sight,
Leave you no eyes but to see misery,
And of your owne, nor speach but to wish thus
Would I had perish'd in the prisons jawes: 455
From whence I was redeem'd! twill weare you old,
Before you have experience in that Art,
That causes your affliction.
CHARALOIS.   Thou dost strike
A deathfull coldnesse to my harts high heate,   460
And shrinkst my liver like the *Calenture.*
Declare this foe of mine, and lifes, that like
A man I may encounter and subdue it,
It shall not have one such effect in mee,
As thou denouncest: with a Souldiers arme,   465
If it be strength, Ile meet it: if a fault
Belonging to my mind, Ile cut it off
With mine owne reason, as a Scholler should.
Speake, though it make mee monstrous.
ROMONT.   Ile dye first.   470
Farewell, continue merry, and high Heaven
Keepe your wife chaste.
CHARALOIS.   Hump, stay and take this wolfe
Out of my brest, that thou hast lodg'd there, or
For ever lose mee.   475
ROMONT.   Lose not, Sir, your selfe.
And I will venture—So the dore is fast.

                              Lockes the dore.

Now noble *Charaloys,* collect your selfe,
Summon your spirits, muster all your strength
That can belong to man, sift passion,   480
From every veine, and whatsoever ensues,
Upbraid not me heereafter, as the cause of
Jealousy, discontent, slaughter and ruine:
Make me not parent to sinne: you will know
This secret that I burne with.   485
CHARALOIS.   Divell on't,
What should it be? *Romont,* I heare you wish
My wifes continuance of Chastity.

ROMONT.   There was no hurt in that.

CHARALOIS.   Why? do you know a likelyhood or possibility   490
Unto the contrarie?

ROMONT.   I know it not, but doubt it, these the grounds
The servant of your wife now young *Novall*,
The sonne unto your fathers Enemy
(Which aggravates my presumption the more)   495
I have bin warnd of, touching her, nay, seene them
Tye heart to heart, one in anothers armes,
Multiplying kisses, as if they meant
To pose Arithmeticke, or whose eyes would
Bee first burnt out, with gazing on the others.   500
I saw their mouthes engender, and their palmes
Glew'd, as if Love had lockt them, their words flow
And melt each others, like two circling flames,
Where chastity, like a Phœnix (me thought) burn'd,
But left the world nor ashes, nor an heire.   505
Why stand you silent thus? what cold dull flegme,
As if you had no drop of choller mixt
In your whole constitution, thus prevailes,
To fix you now, thus stupid hearing this?

CHARALOIS.   You did not see 'em on my Couch within,   510
Like George a horse-back, on her, nor a bed?

ROMONT.   Noe.

CHARALOIS.   Ha, ha.

ROMONT.   Laugh yee? eene so did your wife,
And her indulgent father.   515

CHARALOIS.   They were wise.
Wouldst ha me be a foole?

ROMONT.   No, but a man.

CHARALOIS.   There is no dramme of manhood to suspect,
On such thin ayrie circumstance as this   520
Meere complement and courtship. Was this tale
The hydeous monster which you so conceal'd?
Away, thou curious impertinent
And idle searcher of such leane nice toyes.
Goe, thou sedicious sower of debate: 525
Fly to such matches, where the bridegroome doubts:
He holds not worth enough to countervaile

The vertue and the beauty of his wife.
Thou buzzing drone that 'bout my eares dost hum,
To strike thy rankling sting into my heart,　　　　530
Whose venom, time, nor medicine could asswage.
Thus doe I put thee off, and confident
In mine owne innocency, and desert,
Dare not conceive her so unreasonable,
To put *Novall* in ballance against me,　　　　535
An upstart cran'd up to the height he has.
Hence busiebody, thou'rt no friend to me,
That must be kept to a wives injury.

ROMONT.　　Ist possible? farewell, fine, honest man,
Sweet temper'd Lord adieu: what Apoplexy　　　　540
Hath knit sense up? Is this *Romonts* reward?
Beare witnes the great spirit of thy father,
With what a healthfull hope I administer
This potion that hath wrought so virulently,
I not accuse thy wife of act, but would　　　　545
Prevent her *Præcipuce*, to thy dishonour,
Which now thy tardy sluggishnesse will admit.
Would I had seene thee grav'd with thy great Sire,
Ere live to have mens marginall fingers point
At *Charaloys*, as a lamented story.　　　　550
An Emperour put away his wife for touching
Another man, but thou wouldst have thine tasted
And keepe her (I thinke). Puffe. I am a fire
To warme a dead man, that waste out my selfe.
Bleed—what a plague, a vengeance i'st to mee,　　　　555
If you will be a Cuckold? here I shew
A swords point to thee, this side you may shun,
Or that: the perill, if you will runne on,
I cannot helpe it.

CHARALOIS.　　Didst thou never see me　　　　560
Angry *Romont?*

ROMONT.　　Yes, and pursue a foe
Like lightening.

CHARALOIS.　　Prethee see me so no more.
I can be so againe. Put up thy sword,　　　　565
And take thy selfe away, lest I draw mine.

ROMONT.   Come fright your foes with this: sir, I am your friend,
  And dare stand by you thus.
CHARALOIS.   Thou art not my friend,
  Or being so, thou art mad, I must not buy   570
  Thy friendship at this rate; had I just cause,
  Thou knowst I durst pursue such injury
  Through fire, ayre, water, earth, nay, were they all
  Shuffled againe to *Chaos*, but ther's none.
  Thy skill, *Romont*, consists in camps, not courts.   575
  Farewell, uncivill man, let's meet no more.
  Heere our long web of friendship I untwist.
  Shall I goe whine, walke pale, and locke my wife
  For nothing, from her births free liberty,
  That open'd mine to me? yes; if I doe   580
  The name of cuckold then, dog me with scorne.
  I am a *Frenchman*, no *Italian* borne.

                                                                    Exit.

ROMONT.   A dull *Dutch* rather: fall and coole (my blood)
  Boyle not in zeale of thy friends hurt, so high,
  That is so low, and cold himselfe in't. Woman,   585
  How strong art thou, how easily beguild?
  How thou dost racke us by the very hornes?
  Now wealth I see change manners and the man:
  Something I must do mine owne wrath to asswage,
  And note my friendship to an after-age.   590

                                                                    Exit.

ACT IV

SCENE I

Enter YOUNG NOVALL, *as newly dressed, a* TAYLOR,
  BARBER, PERFUMER, LILADAM, AYMER, PAGE.

YOUNG NOVALL.   Mend this a little: pox! thou hast burnt me.
  Oh fie upon't, O Lard, hee has made me smell (for all the world)
  like a flaxe, or a red headed womans chamber: powder, powder,
  powder.

Novall sits in a chaire, Barber orders his haire, Perfumer
gives powder, Taylor sets his clothese.

PERFUMER.   Oh sweet Lord!   5
PAGE.   That's his Perfumer.
TAYLOR.   Oh deare Lord!
PAGE.   That's his Taylor.
YOUNG NOVALL.   *Monsieur Liladam, Aymour,* how allow you
  the modell of these clothes?   10
AYMER.   Admirably, admirably, oh sweet Lord! assuredly it's
  pitty the wormes should eate thee.
PAGE.   Here's a fine Coil; a Lord, a Taylor, a Perfumer, a Barber,
  and a paire of *Mounsieurs*: 3 to 3? as little wit in the one, as
  honesty in the other. S'foote ile into the country againe, learne 15
  to speake truth, drink Ale, and converse with my fathers
  Tenants; here I heare nothing all day, but upon my soule as I am
  a Gentleman, and an honest man.
AYMER.   I vow and affirme, your Taylor must needs be an expert
  Geometrician, he has the Longitude, Latitude, Altitude, Pro-   20
  fundity, every Demension of your body, so exquisitely, here's a
  lace layd as directly, as if truth were a Taylor.
PAGE.   That were a miracle.
LILADAM.   With a haire breadth's errour, ther's a shoulder
  piece cut, and the base of a pickadille in *puncto*.   25
AYMER.   You are right, Monsieur his vestments fit: as if they
  grew upon him, or art had wrought 'em on the same loome as
  nature fram'd his Lordship, as if your Taylor were deeply read in
  Astrology, and had taken measure of your honourable body, with
  a *Jacobs* staffe, an *Ephimerides*.   30
TAYLOR.   I am bound t'ee Gentlemen.
PAGE.   You are deceiv'd, they'l be bound to you, you must
  remember to trust 'em none.
YOUNG NOVALL.   Nay, fayth, thou art a reasonable neat Arti-
  ficer, give the divell his due.   35
PAGE.   I, if hee would but cut the coate according to the cloth still.
YOUNG NOVALL.   I now want onely my mistres approbation,
  who is indeed, the most polite punctuall Queene of dressing in all

IV. I. 13 Coil] Cell Q. L's emendation.
  14 wit] will Q.

Burgundy. Pah, and makes all other young Ladies appeare, as if
they came from boord last weeke out of the country, Is't not   40
true, *Liladam?*

LILADAM.   True my Lord, as if any thing your Lordship could
say, could be otherwise then true.

YOUNG NOVALL.   Nay a my soule, 'tis so, what fouler object in
the world, then to see a young faire, handsome beauty, unhand-   45
somely dighted and incongruently accoutred; or a hopefull
Chevalier, unmethodically appointed, in the externall ornaments
of nature? For even as the Index tels us the contents of stories,
and directs to the particular Chapters, even so does the outward
habit and superficiall order of garments (in man or woman) give   50
us a tast of the spirit, and demonstratively poynt (as it were a
manuall note from the margin) all the internall quality, and
habiliment of the soule, and there cannot be a more evident, palp-
able, grosse manifestation of poore degenerate dunghilly blood,
and breeding, then rude, unpolish'd, disordered and slovenly   55
outside.

PAGE.   An admirable lecture! Oh all you gallants, that hope to be
saved by your cloathes, edify, edify.

AYMER.   By the Lard, sweet Lard, thou deserv'st a pension o'the
State.   60

PAGE.   Oth'Taylors, two such Lords were able to spread Taylors
ore the face of a whole kingdome.

YOUNG NOVALL.   Pox a this glasse! it flatters, I could find in my
heart to breake it.

PAGE.   O save the glasse my Lord, and breake their heads, they   65
are the greater flatterers I assure you.

AYMER.   Flatters—detracts, impayres, yet put it by,
Lest thou deare Lord (*Narcissus*-like) should doate
Upon thy selfe, and dye; and rob the world
Of natures copy, that she workes forme by.   70

LILADAM.   Oh that I were the Infanta Queene of Europe,
Who (but thy selfe sweete Lord) shouldst marry me.

YOUNG NOVALL.   I marry? were there a Queene oth'world,
not I.

He capers.

Wedlocke? no padlocke, horslocke, I weare spurrs   75

To keepe it off my heeles; yet my *Aymour*,
Like a free wanton jennet i'th meddows,
I looke about, and neigh, take hedge and ditch,
Feed in my neighbours pastures, picke my choyce
Of all their faire-maind-mares: but married once,   80
A man is stak'd, or pown'd, and cannot graze
Beyond his owne hedge.

Enter PONTALIER, *and* MALOTIN.

PONTALIER.   I have waited, sir,
Three houres to speake w'ee, and not take it well,
Such magpies, are admitted, whilst I daunce   85
Attendance.
LILADAM.   Magpies? what d'ee take me for?
PONTALIER.   A long thing with a most unpromising face.
AYMER.   I'll ne're aske him, what he takes me for!
MALOTIN.   Doe not, sir,   90
For hee'l goe neere to tell you.
PONTALIER.   Art not thou a Barber Surgeon?
BARBER.   Yes sira why?
PONTALIER.   My Lord is sorely troubled with two scabs.
LILADAM. AYMER.   Humph—   95
PONTALIER.   I prethee cure him of 'em.
YOUNG NOVALL.   Pish: no more,
Thy gall sure's overthrowne; these are my Councell,
And we were now in serious discourse.
PONTALIER.   Of perfume and apparell, can you rise   100
And spend 5 houres in dressing talke, with these?
YOUNG NOVALL.   Thou'ldst have me be a dog: up, stretch and
shake,
And ready for all day.
PONTALIER.   Sir, would you be   105
More curious in preserving of your honour
Trim, 'twere more manly. I am come to wake
Your reputation, from this lethargy
You let it sleepe in, to perswade, importune,
Nay, to provoke you, sir, to call to account   110
This Collonell *Romont*, for the foule wrong
Which like a burthen, he hath layd on you,

And like a drunken porter, you sleepe under.
'Tis all the towne talkes, and beleeve, sir,
If your tough sence persist thus, you are undone,   115
Utterly lost, you will be scornd and baffled
By every Lacquay; season now your youth,
With one brave thing, and it shall keep the odour
Even to your death, beyond, and on your Tombe,
Sent like sweet oyles and Frankincense; sir, this life   120
Which once you sav'd, I ne're since counted mine,
I borrow'd it of you; and now will pay it;
I tender you the service of my sword
To beare your challenge: if you'l write, your fate
I'le make mine owne: what ere betide you, I   125
That have liv'd by you, by your side will dye.
YOUNG NOVALL.   Ha, ha, would'st ha' me challenge poore
  Romont?
Fight with close breeches, thou mayst thinke I dare not.
Doe not mistake me (cooze) I am very valiant,   130
But valour shall not make me such an Asse.
What use is there of valour (now a dayes?)
'Tis sure, or to be kill'd, or to be hang'd.
Fight thou as thy minde moves thee, 'tis thy trade,
Thou hast nothing else to doe; fight with *Romont?*   135
No, i'le not fight under a Lord.
PONTALIER.   Farewell, sir, I pitty you.
Such loving Lords walke their dead honours graves,
For no companions fit, but fooles and knaves.
Come *Malotin.*   140

Exeunt PONTALIER, MALOTIN.

Enter ROMONT.

LILADAM.   'Sfoot, *Colbran,* the low gyant.
AYMER.   He has brought a battaile in his face, let's goe.
PAGE.   *Colbran* d'ee call him? hee'l make some of you smoake, I
  beleeve.
ROMONT.   By your leave, sirs.   145
AYMER.   Are you a Consort?
ROMONT.   D'ee take me for
  A fidler? ya're deceiv'd: looke. Ile pay you.   *Kickes 'em.*

PAGE.   It seemes he knows you one, he bumfiddles you so.

LILADAM.   Was there ever so base a fellow?   150

AYMER.   A rascall?

LILADAM.   A most uncivill Groome?

AYMER.   Offer to kicke a Gentleman, in a Noblemans chamber?
A pox of your manners.

LILADAM.   Let him alone, let him alone, thou shalt lose thy arme,   155
fellow: if wee stirre against thee, hang us.

PAGE.   S'foote, I thinke they have the better on him, though
they be kickd, they talke so.

LILADAM.   Let's leave the mad Ape.

YOUNG NOVALL.   Gentlemen.   160

LILADAM.   Nay, my Lord, we will not offer to dishonour you so
much as to stay by you, since hee's alone.

YOUNG NOVALL.   Harke you.

AYMER.   We doubt the cause, and will not disparage you, so
much as to take your Lordships quarrell in hand. Plague on him,   165
how he has crumpled our bands.

PAGE.   Ile eene away with 'em, for this souldier beates man,
woman, and child.

Exeunt. Manent NOVALL, ROMONT.

YOUNG NOVALL.   What meane you, sir? My people.

ROMONT.   Your boye's gone,   *Lockes the doore.* 170
And doore's lockt, yet for no hurt to you,
But privacy: call up your blood againe, sir, be not afraid, I do
Beseech you, sir, (and therefore come) without more circumstance
Tell me how farre the passages have gone
'Twixt you, and your faire Mistresse *Beaumelle.*   175
Tell me the truth, and by my hope of Heaven
It never shall goe further.

YOUNG NOVALL.   Tell you why sir?
Are you my confessor?

ROMONT.   I will be your confounder, if you doe not.   180

Drawes a pocket dag.

Stirre not, nor spend your voyce.

YOUNG NOVALL.   What will you doe?

ROMONT.   Nothing but lyne your brayne-pan, sir, with lead,

If you not satisfie me suddenly,
I am desperate of my life, and command yours.   185
YOUNG NOVALL.   Hold, hold, ile speake. I vow to heaven and
you,
Shee's yet untouch't, more then her face and hands:
I cannot call her innocent, for I yeeld
On my sollicitous wooing she consented   190
Where time and place met oportunity
To grant me all requests.
ROMONT.   But may I build on this assurance?

                              Drawes Inkhorne and paper.

YOUNG NOVALL.   As upon your fayth.
ROMONT.   Write this, sir, nay you must.   195
YOUNG NOVALL.   Pox of this Gunne.
ROMONT.   Withall, sir, you must sweare, and put your oath
Under your hand, (shake not) ne're to frequent
This Ladies company, nor ever send
Token, or message, or letter, to incline   200
This (too much prone already) yeelding Lady.
YOUNG NOVALL.   'Tis done, sir.
ROMONT.   Let me see, this first is right,
And here you wish a sudden death may light
Upon your body, and hell take your soule,   205
If ever more you see her, but by chance,
Much lesse allure her. Now, my Lord, your hand.
YOUNG NOVALL.   My hand to this?
ROMONT.   Your heart else I assure you.
YOUNG NOVALL.   Nay, there 'tis.   210
ROMONT.   So keepe this last article
Of your fayth given, and stead of threatnings, sir,
The service of my sword and life is yours:
But not a word of it, 'tis Fairies treasure;
Which but reveal'd, brings on the blabbers, ruine.   215
Use your youth better, and this excellent forme
Heaven hath bestowed upon you. So good morrow to your
Lordship.
                                                    Exit.

                    190 wooing] wrongs Q.

YOUNG NOVALL.   Good divell to your rogueship. No man's
   safe: 220
Ile have a Cannon planted in my chamber,
Against such roaring roagues.

Enter BELLAPERT.

BELLAPERT.   My Lord away
   The Coach stayes: now have your wish, and judge,
If I have beene forgetfull.   225
YOUNG NOVALL.   Ha?
BELLAPERT.   D'ee stand
Humming and hawing now?

                                                       Exit.

YOUNG NOVALL.   Sweete wench, I come.
   Hence feare,   230
I swore, that's all one, my next oath 'ile keepe
That I did meane to breake, and then 'tis quit.
No paine is due to lovers perjury.
If Jove himselfe laugh at it, so will I.

                                         Exit NOVALL.

SCENE II

Enter CHARALOIS, BEAUMONT.

BEAUMONT.   I grieve for the distaste, though I have manners,
   Not to inquire the cause, falne out betweene
Your Lordship and *Romont*.
CHARALOIS.   I love a friend,
   So long as he continues in the bounds   5
Prescrib'd by friendship, but when he usurpes
Too farre on what is proper to my selfe,
And puts the habit of a Governor on,
I must and will preserve my liberty.
But speake of something else, this is a theame   10
I take no pleasure in: what's this *Aymeire*,
Whose voyce for Song, and excellent knowledge in
The chiefest parts of Musique, you bestow
Such prayses on?

234 Jove] love Q.

BEAUMONT.   He is a Gentleman,   15
  (For so his quality speakes him) well receiv'd
  Among our greatest Gallants; but yet holds
  His maine dependance from the young Lord *Novall*:
  Some trickes and crochets he has in his head,
  As all Musicians have, and more of him   20
  I dare not author: but when you have heard him,
  I may presume, your Lordship so will like him,
  That you'l hereafter be a friend to Musique.
CHARALOIS.   I never was an enemy to't, *Baumont*,
  Nor yet doe I subscribe to the opinion   25
  Of those old Captaines, that thought nothing musicall,
  But cries of yeelding enemies, neighing of horses,
  Clashing of armour, lowd shouts, drums, and trumpets:
  Nor on the other side in favour of it,
  Affirme the world was made by musicall discord,   30
  Or that the happinesse of our life consists
  In a well varied note upon the Lute:
  I love it to the worth of it, and no further.
  But let us see this wonder.
BEAUMONT.   He prevents my calling of him.   35

Enter AYMER.

AYMER.   Let the Coach be brought
  To the backe gate, and serve the banquet up:
  My good Lord *Charalois*, I thinke my house
  Much honor'd in your presence.
CHARALOIS.   To have meanes,   40
  To know you better, sir, has brought me hither
  A willing visitant, and you'l crowne my welcome
  In making me a witnesse to your skill,
  Which crediting from others I admire.
AYMER.   Had I beene one houre sooner made acquainted   45
  With your intent my Lord, you should have found me
  Better provided: now such as it is,
  Pray you grace with your acceptance.
BEAUMONT.   You are modest.
AYMER.   Begin the last new ayre.   50
CHARALOIS.   Shall we not see them?

AYMER.   This little distance from the instruments
   Will to your eares convey the harmony
   With more delight.
CHARALOIS.   Ile not consent.   55
AYMER. ⟨*Aside.*⟩   Y'are tedious,
   By this meanes shall I with one banquet please
   Two companies, those within and these Guls heere.

                                                      Song above.

            Citizens Song of the Courtier.

         Courtier, if thou needs wilt wive,
         From this lesson learne to thrive.   60
         If thou match a Lady, that
         Passes thee in birth and state,
         Let her curious garments be
         Twice above thine owne degree;
         This will draw great eyes upon her,   65
         Get her servants and thee honour.

   ⟨*During*⟩ *Song, Beaumelle* ⟨*is heard*⟩ *within,* ⟨*laughing*⟩.

CHARALOIS. ⟨*Aside.*⟩   How's this? It is my Ladies laugh! most
   certaine
   When I first pleas'd her, in this merry language,
   She gave me thanks.
BEAUMONT.   How like you this?   70
CHARALOIS.   'Tis rare—
   ⟨*Aside.*⟩ Yet I may be deceiv'd, and should be sorry
   Upon uncertaine suppositions, rashly
   To write my selfe in the blacke list of those
   I have declaym'd against, and to *Romont.*   75
AYMER. ⟨*Aside.*⟩   I would he were well of—perhaps your
   Lordship
   Likes not these sad tunes, I have a new Song
   Set to a lighter note, may please you better;
   'Tis cal'd The happy husband.
CHARALOIS.   Pray sing it.   80

                                                      Song below.

IV. II. 66 S.D. Q reads: *"Musique and a Song, Beaumelle within—ha, ha, ha."*

Courtiers Song of the Citizen

Poore Citizen, if thou wilt be
A happy husband, learne of me;
To set thy wife first in thy shop,
A faire wife, a kinde wife, a sweet wife, sets a poore man up.
What though thy shelves be ne're so bare:　　　　85
A woman still is currant ware:
Each man will cheapen, foe, and friend,
But whilst thou art at tother end,
What ere thou seest, or what dost heare,
Foole, have no eye to, nor an eare;　　　　90
And after supper for her sake,
When thou hast fed, snort, though thou wake:
What though the Gallants call thee mome?
Yet with thy lanthorne light her home:
Then looke into the towne and tell,　　　　95
If no such Tradesmen there doe dwell.

At the end of the Song, Beaumelle within.

BEAUMELLE.　Ha, ha, 'tis such a groome.
CHARALOIS.　Doe I heare this, and yet stand doubtfull?

Exit CHARALOIS.

AYMER.　Stay him I am undone,
　　And they discovered.　　　　100
BEAUMONT.　Whats the matter?
AYMER.　Ah!
　　That women, when they are well pleas'd, cannot hold,
　　But must laugh out.

Enter YOUNG NOVALL, CHARALOIS, BEAUMELLE,
　　BELLAPERT.

YOUNG NOVALL.　Helpe, save me, murther, murther.　　　　105
BEAUMELLE.　Undone forever.
CHARALOIS.　Oh, my heart!
　　Hold yet a little—doe not hope to scape
　　By flight, it is impossible: though I might
　　On all advantage take thy life, and justly;　　　　110
　　This sword, my fathers sword, that here was drawne,
　　But to a noble purpose, shall not now

Doe th'office of a hangman, I reserve it
To right mine honour, not for a revenge
So poore, that though with thee, it should cut off   115
Thy family, with all that are allyed
To thee in lust, or basenesse, 'twere still short of
All termes of satisfaction. Draw.
YOUNG NOVALL.   I dare not,
I have already done you too much wrong,   120
To fight in such a cause.
CHARALOIS.   Why, darest thou neyther
Be honest, coward, nor yet valiant, knave?
In such a cause come doe not shame thy selfe:
Such whose bloods wrongs, or wrong done to themselves   125
Could never heate, are yet in the defence
Of their whores daring, looke on her againe.
You thought her worth the hazard of your soule,
And yet stand doubtfull in her quarrell, to
Venture your body.   130
BEAUMONT.   No, he feares his cloaths, more then his flesh.
CHARALOIS.   Keepe from me, garde thy life,
Or as thou hast liv'd like a goate, thou shalt
Dye like a sheepe.
YOUNG NOVALL.   Since ther's no remedy   135
Despaire of safety now in me prove courage.

They fight, Novall is slaine.

CHARALOIS.   How soone weak wrong's or'throwne! lend me
your hand,
Beare this to the Caroach—come, you have taught me
To say you must and shall: I wrong you not,
Y'are but to keepe him company you love.   140
Is't done? 'tis well. Raise officers, and take care,
All you can apprehend within the house
May be forthcomming. Do I appeare much mov'd?
BEAUMONT.   No, sir.
CHARALOIS.   My griefes are now, Thus to be borne   145
Hereafter ile finde time and place to mourne.

Exeunt.

SCENE III

Enter ROMONT, PONTALIER.

PONTALIER.   I was bound to seeke you, sir.
ROMONT.   And had you found me
  In any place, but in the streete, I should
  Have done,—not talk'd to you. Are you the Captaine?
  The hopefull *Pontalier?* whom I have seene   5
  Doe in the field such service, as then made you
  Their envy that commanded, here at home
  To play the parasite to a gilded knave,
  And it may be the Pander.
PONTALIER.   Without this   10
  I come to call you to account, for what
  Is past already. I by your example
  Of thankfulnesse to the dead Generall
  By whom you were rais'd, have practis'd to be so
  To my good Lord *Novall,* by whom I live;   15
  Whose least disgrace that is, or may be offred,
  With all the hazzard of my life and fortunes,
  I will make good on you, or any man,
  That has a hand in't; and since you allowe me
  A Gentleman and a souldier, there's no doubt   20
  You will except against me. You shall meete
  With a faire enemy, you understand
  The right I looke for, and must have.
ROMONT.   I doe,
  And with the next dayes sunne you shall heare from me.   25

                               Exeunt.

SCENE IV

Enter CHARALOIS *with a casket,* BEAUMELLE, BEAUMONT.

CHARALOIS.   Pray beare this to my father, at his leisure
  He may persue it: but with your best language

Intreat his instant presence: you have sworne
Not to reveale what I have done.

BEAUMONT.   Nor will I—but—   5

CHARALOIS.   Doubt me not, by Heaven, I will doe nothing
But what may stand with honour: Pray you leave me
To my owne thoughts. If this be to me, rise;

⟨*Exit* BEAUMONT.⟩

I am not worthy the looking on, but onely
To feed contempt and scorne, and that from you   10
Who with the losse of your faire name have caus'd it,
Were too much cruelty.

BEAUMELLE.   I dare not move you
To heare me speake. I know my fault is farre
Beyond qualification, or excuse,   15
That 'tis not fit for me to hope, or you
To thinke of mercy; onely I presume
To intreate, you would be pleas'd to looke upon
My sorrow for it, and beleeve, these teares
Are the true children of my griefe and not   20
A womans cunning.

CHARALOIS.   Can you *Beaumelle*,
Having deceived so great a trust as mine,
Though I were all credulity, hope againe
To get beleefe? no, no, if you looke on me   25
With pity or dare practise any meanes
To make my sufferings lesse, or give just cause
To all the world, to thinke what I must doe,
Was cal'd upon by you, use other waies,
Deny what I have seene, or justifie   30
What you have done, and as you desperately
Made shipwracke of your fayth to be a whore,
Use th' armes of such a one, and such defence,
And multiply the sinne, with impudence,
Stand boldly up, and tell me to my teeth,   35
You have done but what's warranted,
By great examples, in all places, where
Women inhabit; urge your owne deserts,
Or want of me in merit; tell me how,

Your dowre from the low gulfe of poverty,   40
Weighd up my fortunes, to what now they are:
That I was purchas'd by your choyse, and practise,
To shelter you from shame; that you might sinne
As boldly as securely: that poore men
Are married to those wives that bring them wealth,   45
One day their husbands, but observers ever:
That when by this prov'd usage you have blowne
The fire of my just vengeance to the height,
I then may kill you: and say 'twas done
In heate of blood, and after die my selfe,   50
To witnesse my repentance.

BEAUMELLE.   O my fate,
That never would consent that I should see,
How worthy thou wert both of love and duty
Before I lost you; and my misery made   55
The glasse, in which I now behold your vertue:
While I was good, I was a part of you,
And of two, by the vertuous harmony
Of our faire mindes, made one: but since I wandred
In the forbidden Labyrinth of lust,   60
What was inseparable, is by me divided.
With justice therefore you may cut me off,
And from your memory, wash the remembrance
That ere I was, like to some vicious purpose
Within your better judgement, you repent of   65
And study to forget.

CHARALOIS.   O *Beaumelle*,
That you can speake so well, and doe so ill!
But you had bin too great a blessing, if
You had continued chast: see how you force me   70
To this, because mine honour will not yeeld
That I againe should love you.

BEAUMELLE.   In this life
It is not fit you should: yet you shall finde,
Though I was bold enough to be a strumpet,   75

IV. IV 47 Prov'd] prou'd Q. An insoluble crux. While edd. have inclined to
favour reading "proud" here, the text must stand, since emendation is purely
subjective.

I dare not yet live one: let those fam'd matrones
That are canoniz'd worthy of our sex,
Transcend me in their sanctity of life,
I yet will equall them in dying nobly,
Ambitious of no honour after life,   80
But that when I am dead, you will forgive me.
CHARALOIS.   How pity steales upon me! should I heare her

Knock within.

But ten words more, I were lost—one knocks, go in.
That to be mercifull should be a sinne.

Exit BEAUMELLE.

Enter ROCHFORT.

O, sir, most welcome. Let me take your cloake,   85
I must not be denyed—here are your robes,
As you love justice once more put them on:
There is a cause to be determind of
That doe's require such an integrity,
As you have ever us'd—ile put you to   90
The tryall of your constancy, and goodnesse:
And looke that you that have beene Eagle-eyd
In other mens affaires, prove not a Mole
In what concernes your selfe. Take you your seate:
I will be for you presently.   95

Exit ⟨CHARALOIS.⟩

ROCHFORT.   Angels guard me,
To what strange Tragedy does this destraction
Serve for a Prologue?

Enter CHARALOIS, *with Novals body.* BEAUMELLE, BEAUMONT.

CHARALOIS.   So, set it downe before
The Judgement seate, and stand you at the bar: 100
For me? I am the accuser.
ROCHFORT.   *Novall* slayne,
And *Beaumelle* my daughter in the place
Of one to be arraign'd.

---

97 destraction] destruction Q, indication (sugg. by M, adopted by G). M's emendation is attractive, but difficult to justify textually: "destruction" is surely wrong.

CHARALOIS.   O, are you touch'd?   105
 I finde that I must take an other course,
 Feare nothing. I will onely blinde your eyes,

         ⟨*Blindfolds him.*⟩

 For Justice should do so, when 'tis to meete
 An object that may sway her equall doome
 From what it should be aim'd at.—Good my Lord,   110
 A day of hearing.
ROCHFORT.   It is granted, speake—you shall have justice.
CHARALOIS.   I then here accuse,
 Most equall Judge, the prisoner your faire Daughter.
 For whom I owed so much to you: your daughter,   115
 So worthy in her owne parts: and that worth
 Set forth by yours, to whose so rare perfections,
 Truth witnesse with me, in the place of service
 I almost pay'd Idolatrous sacrifice
 To be a false adultresse.   120
ROCHFORT.   With whom?
CHARALOIS.   With this *Novall* here dead.
ROCHFORT.   Be wel advis'd
 And ere you say adultresse againe,
 Her fame depending on it, be most sure   125
 That she is one.
CHARALOIS.   I tooke them in the act.
 I know no proofe beyond it.
ROCHFORT.   O my heart.
CHARALOIS.   A Judge should feele no passions.   130
ROCHFORT.   Yet remember
 He is a man, and cannot put off nature.
 What answere makes the prisoner?
BEAUMELLE.   I confesse
 The fact I am charg'd with, and yeeld my selfe   135
 Most miserably guilty.
ROCHFORT.   Heaven take mercy
 Upon your soule then: it must leave your body.
 Now free mine eyes, I dare unmov'd looke on her,
 And fortifie my sentence, with strong reasons.   140
 Since that the politique law provides that servants,

To whose care we commit our goods shall die,
If they abuse our trust: what can you looke for,
To whose charge this most hopefull Lord gave up
All hee receiv'd from his brave Ancestors,   145
Or he could leave to his posterity?
His Honour, wicked woman, in whose safety
All his lifes joyes, and comforts were locked up,
With thy lust, a theefe hath now stolne from him,
And therefore—   150

CHARALOIS.   Stay, just Judge, may not what's lost
By her one fault, (for I am charitable,
And charge her not with many) be forgotten
In her faire life hereafter?

ROCHFORT.   Never, Sir.   155
The wrong that's done to the chaste married bed,
Repentant teares can never expiate,
And be assured, to pardon such a sinne,
Is an offence as great as to commit it.

CHARALOIS.   I may not then forgive her.   160

ROCHFORT.   Nor she hope it.
Nor can shee wish to live: no sunne shall rise,
But ere it set, shall shew her ugly lust
In a new shape, and every one more horrid:
Nay, even those prayers, which with such humble fervour   165
She seemes to send up yonder, are beate backe,
And all suites, which her penitence can proffer,
As soone as made, are with contempt throwne
Off all the courts of mercy.

CHARALOIS.   Let her die then.

                                        He kils her.

Better prepar'd I am. Sure I could not take her,   170
Nor she accuse her father, as a Judge
Partiall against her.

BEAUMELLE.   I approve his sentence,
And kisse the executioner: my lust   175
Is now run from me in that blood in which
It was begot and nourished.

ROCHFORT.   Is she dead then?

CHARALOIS.   Yes, sir, this is her heart blood, is it not?
  I thinke it be.   180
ROCHFORT.   And you have kild her?
CHARALOIS.   True, and did it by your doome.
ROCHFORT.   But I pronounc'd it
  As a Judge onely, and friend to justice,
  And zealous in defence of your wrong'd honour,   185
  Broke all the tyes of nature: and cast off
  The love and soft affection of a father.
  I in your cause, put on a Scarlet robe
  Of red died cruelty, but in returne,
  You have advanc'd for me no flag of mercy: 190
  I look'd on you, as a wrong'd husband, but
  You clos'd your eyes against me, as a father.
  O *Beaumelle*, my daughter.
CHARALOIS.   This is madnesse.
ROCHFORT.   Keep from me—could not one good thought rise up,   195
  To tell you that she was my ages comfort,
  Begot by a weake man, and borne a woman,
  And could not therefore, but partake of frailety?
  Or wherefore did not thankfulnesse step forth,
  To urge my many merits, which I may   200
  Object unto you, since you prove ungratefull,
  Flinty-hearted *Charaloys*?
CHARALOIS.   Nature does prevaile above your vertue.
ROCHFORT.   No: it gives me eyes,
  To pierce the heart of designe against me.   205
  I finde it now, it was my state was aym'd at,
  A nobler match was sought for, and the houres
  I liv'd, grew teadious to you: my compassion
  Towards you hath rendred me most miserable,
  And foolish charity undone my selfe: 210
  But ther's a Heaven above, from whose just wreake
  No mists of policy can hide offendors.

Enter NOVALL SENIOR *with* OFFICERS.

NOVALL SENIOR.   Force ope the doors—O monster, caniball,
  Lay hold on him, my sonne, my sonne.—O *Rochfort*,
  'Twas you gave liberty to this bloody wolfe   215

To worry all our comforts,—But this is
No time to quarrell: now give your assistance
For the revenge.
ROCHFORT.   Call it a fitter name—Justice for innocent blood.
CHARALOIS.   Though all conspire   220
Against that life which I am weary of,
A little longer yet ile strive to keepe it,
To shew in spite of malice, and their lawes,
His plea must speed that hath an honest cause.

                                        Exeunt.

ACT V

SCENE I

Enter LILADAM, TAYLOR, OFFICERS.

LILADAM.   Why 'tis both most unconscionable, and untimely
T'arrest a gallant for his cloaths, before
He has worne them out: besides you sayd you ask'd
My name in my Lords bond but for forme onely,
And now you'l lay me up for't. Do not thinke   5
The taking measure of a customer
By a brace of varlets, though I rather wait
Never so patiently, will prove a fashion
Which any Courtier or Innes of court man
Would follow willingly.   10
TAYLOR.   There I beleeve you.
But sir, I must have present moneys, or
Assurance to secure me, when I shall.—
Or I will see to your comming forth.
LILADAM.   Plague on't,   15
You have provided for my enterance in:
That comming forth you talke of, concernes me.
What shall I doe? you have done me a disgrace
In the arrest, but more in giving cause
To all the street, to thinke I cannot stand   20
Without these two supporters for my armes:
                    v. i. 4 for forme] for me Q.

Pray you let them loose me: for their satisfaction
I will not run away.
TAYLOR.   For theirs you will not,
But for your owne you would; looke to them fellows.   25
LILADAM.   Why doe you call them fellows? doe not wrong
Your reputation so, as you are meerely
A Taylor, faythfull, apt to beleeve in Gallants
You are a companion at a ten crowne supper
For cloth of bodkin, and may with one Larke   30
Eate up three manchets, and no man observe you,
Or call your trade in question for't. But when
You study your debt-booke, and hold correspondence
With officers of the hanger, and leave swordmen,
The learned conclude, the Taylor and Sergeant   35
In the expression of a knave and thefe
To be *Synonima*. Looke therefore to it,
And let us part in peace, I would be loth
You should undoe your selfe.

Enter NOVALL SENIOR *and* PONTALIER.

TAYLOR.   To let you goe   40
Were the next way.
But see! heeres your old Lord,
Let him but give his word I shall be paide,
And you are free.
LILADAM.   S'lid, I will put him to't: 45
I can be but denied: or what say you?
His Lordship owing me three times your debt,
If you arrest him at my suite, and let me
Goe run before to see the action entred.
'Twould be a witty jest.   50
TAYLOR.   I must have ernest:
I cannot pay my debts so.
PONTALIER.   Can your Lordship
Imagine, while I live and weare a sword,
Your sonnes death shall be unreveng'd?   55
NOVALL SENIOR.   I know not
One reason why you should not doe like others:

55 unreveng'd] reueng'd Q.

I am sure, of all the herd that fed upon him,
I cannot see in any, now hee's gone,
In pitty or in thankfulnesse one true signe   60
Of sorrow for him.
PONTALIER.   All his bounties yet
Fell not in such unthankefull ground: 'tis true
He had weaknesses, but such as few are free from,
And though none sooth'd them lesse then I: for now   65
To say that I foresaw the dangers that
Would rise from cherishing them, were but untimely.
I yet could wish the justice that you seeke for
In the revenge, had bin trusted to me,
And not the uncertaine issue of the lawes: 70
'Tas rob'd me of a noble testimony
Of what I durst doe for him: but however,
My forfait life redeem'd by him though dead,
Shall doe him service.
NOVALL SENIOR.   As farre as my griefe   75
Will give me leave, I thanke you.
LILADAM.   Oh my Lord,
Oh my good Lord, deliver me from these furies.
PONTALIER.   Arrested? This is one of them whose base
And abject flattery helpt to digge his grave: 80
He is not worth your pitty, nor my anger.
Goe to the basket and repent.
NOVALL SENIOR.   Away! I onely know now to hate thee
deadly:
I will doe nothing for thee.
LILADAM.   Nor you, Captaine?   85
PONTALIER.   No, to your trade againe, put off this case,
It may be the discovering what you were,
When your unfortunate master tooke you up,
May move compassion in your creditor.
Confesse the truth.   90

Exit NOVALL SENIOR, PONTALIER.

LILADAM.   And now I thinke on't better,
I will, brother, your hand, your hand, sweet brother.
I am of your sect, and my gallantry but a dreame,

Out of which these two fearefull apparitions
Against my will have wak'd me. This rich sword   95
Grew suddenly out of a taylors bodkin;
These hangers from my vailes and fees in Hell:
And where as now this beaver sits, full often
A thrifty cape compos'd of broad cloth lists,
Nere kin unto the cushion where I sate   100
Crosse-leg'd, and yet ungartred, hath beene seene,
Our breakefasts famous for the buttred loaves,
I have with joy bin oft acquainted with,
And therefore use a conscience, though it be
Forbidden in our hall towards other men,   105
To me that as I have beene, will againe
Be of the brotherhood.

OFFICER.   I know him now:
He was a prentice to *Le Robe* at *Orleance*.

LILADAM.   And from thence brought by my young Lord, now   110
dead,
Unto *Dijon*, and with him till this houre
Hath bin receiv'd here for a compleate Mounsieur.
Nor wonder at it: for but tythe our gallants,
Even those of the first ranke, and you will finde
In every ten, one: peradventure two,   115
That smell ranke of the dancing schoole, or fiddle,
The pantofle or pressing yron: but hereafter
Weele talke of this. I will surrender up
My suites againe: there cannot be much losse,
'Tis but the turning of the lace, with one   120
Addition more you know of, and what wants
I will worke out.

TAYLOR.   Then here our quarrell ends.
The gallant is turn'd Taylor, and all friends.

Exeunt.

SCENE II

Enter ROMONT, BEAUMONT.

ROMONT.   You have them ready.

BEAUMONT.   Yes, and they will speake
  Their knowledg in this cause, when thou thinkst fit
  To have them cal'd upon.
ROMONT.   'Tis well, and something   5
  I can adde to their evidence, to prove
  This brave revenge, which they would have cal'd murther,
  A noble Justice.
BEAUMONT.   In this you expresse
  (The breach by my Lords want of you, new made up)   10
  A faythfull friend.
ROMONT.   That friendship's rays'd on sand,
  Which every sudden gust of discontent,
  Or flowing of our passions can change,
  As if it nere had bin: but doe you know   15
  Who are to sit on him?
BEAUMONT.   Monsieur *Du Croy*
  Assisted by *Charmi.*
ROMONT.   The Advocate
  That pleaded for the Marshalls funerall,   20
  And was checkt for it by *Novall.*
BEAUMONT.   The same.
ROMONT.   How fortunes that?
BEAUMONT.   Why, sir, my Lord *Novall*
  Being the accuser, cannot be the Judge,   25
  Nor would grievd *Rochfort*, but Lord *Charaloys*
  (How-ever he might wrong him by his power,)
  Should have an equall hearing.
ROMONT.   By my hopes
  Of *Charaloys* acquitall, I lament   30
  That reverent old mans fortune.
BEAUMONT.   Had you seene him,
  As to my griefe I have, now promis'd patience,
  And ere it was beleev'd, though spake by him
  That never brake his word, inrag'd againe   35
  So far as to make warre upon those heires,
  Which not a barbarous Scythian durst presume
  To touch, but with a superstitious feare,
  As something sacred, and then curse his daughter,
  But with more frequent violence himselfe,   40

As if he had bin guilty of her fault,
By being incredulous of your report,
You would not onely judge him worthy pitty,
But suffer with him.

Enter CHARALOIS, *with* OFFICERS.

But heere comes the prisoner,   45
I dare not stay to doe my duty to him,
Yet rest assur'd, all possible meanes in me
To doe him service, keepes you company.

                                        Exit BEAUMONT.

ROMONT.   It is not doubted.
CHARALOIS.   Why, yet as I came hither,   50
  The people apt to mocke calamity,
  And tread on the oppress'd, made no hornes at me,
  Though they are too familiar: I deserve them.
  And knowing what blood my sword had drunke
  In wreake of that disgrace, they yet forbare   55
  To shake their heads, or to revile me for
  A murtherer, they rather all put on
  (As for great losses the old *Romans* us'd)
  A generall face of sorrow, waighted on
  By a sad murmur breaking through their silence,   60
  And no eye but was readier with a teare
  To witnesse 'twas shed for me, then I could
  Discerne a face made up with scorne against me.
  Why should I then, though for unusuall wrongs
  I chose unusuall meanes to right those wrongs,   65
  Condemne my selfe, as over-partiall
  In my owne cause? *Romont*!
ROMONT.   Best friend, well met,
  By my hearts love to you, and joyne to that,
  My thankfulnesse that still lives to the dead,   70
  I looke upon you now with more true joy,
  Then when I saw you married.
CHARALOIS.   You have reason
  To give you warrant for't; my falling off
  From such a friendship with the scorne that answered   75

Your too propheticke counsell, may well move you
To thinke your meeting me going to my death,
A fit encounter for that hate which justly
I have deserv'd from you.

ROMONT.   Shall I still then   80
Speake truth, and be ill understood?

CHARALOIS.   You are not.
I am conscious, I have wrong'd you, and allow me
Onely a morall man—to looke on you,
Whom foolishly I have abus'd and injur'd,   85
Must of necessity be more terrible to me,
Then any death the Judges can pronounce
From the tribunall which I am to plead at.

ROMONT.   Passion transports you.

CHARALOIS.   For what I have done   90
To my false Lady, or *Novall*, I can
Give some apparent cause: but touching you,
In my defence, childlike, I can say nothing,
But I am sorry for't, a poore satisfaction:
And yet mistake me not: for it is more   95
Then I will speake, to have my pardon sign'd
For all I stand accus'd of.

ROMONT.   You much weaken the strength of your good cause.
Should you but thinke
A man for doing well could entertaine   100
A pardon, were it offred, you have given
To blinde and slow-pac'd justice, wings, and eyes
To see and overtake impieties,
Which from a cold proceeding had receiv'd
Indulgence or protection.   105

CHARALOIS.   Thinke you so?

ROMONT.   Upon my soule nor should the blood you chalenged
And tooke to cure your honour, breed more scruple
In your soft conscience, then if your sword
Had bin sheath'd in a Tygre, or she Beare,   110
That in their bowels would have made your tombe.
To injure innocence is more then murther:
But when inhumane lusts transforme us, then
As beasts we are to suffer, not like men

To be lamented. Nor did *Charalois* ever   115
Performe an act so worthy the applause
Of a full theater of perfect men,
As he hath done in this: the glory got
By overthrowing outward enemies,
Since strength and fortune are maine sharers in it,   120
We cannot but by pieces call our owne:
But when we conquer our intestine foes,
Our passions breed within us, and of those
The most rebellious tyrant powerfull love,
Our reason suffering us to like no longer   125
Then the faire object being good deserves it,
That's a true victory, which, were great men
Ambitious to atchieve, by your example
Setting no price upon the breach of fayth,
But losse of life, 'twould fright adultery   130
Out of their families, and make lust appeare
As lothsome to us in the first consent,
As when 'tis wayted on by punishment.

CHARALOIS.   You have confirm'd me. Who would love a woman
That might injoy in such a man, a friend?   135
You have made me know the justice of my cause,
And mark't me out the way, how to defend it.

ROMONT.   Continue to that resolution constant,
And you shall, in contempt of their worst malice,
Come off with honour. Heere they come.   140

CHARALOIS.   I am ready.

Enter DU CROYE, CHARMI, ROCHFORT, NOVALL SENIOR,
PONTALIER, BEAUMONT.

NOVALL SENIOR.   See, equall Judges, with what confidence
The cruel murtherer stands, as if he would
Outface the Court and Justice!

ROCHFORT.   But looke on him,   145
And you shall finde, for still methinks I doe,
Though guilt hath dide him black, something good in him,
That may perhaps worke with a wiser man

v. II. 141 S.D. At this point Q begins Scene III, but location and action are
uninterrupted.

Then I have beene, againe to set him free
And give him all he has.   150
CHARMI.   This is not well.
   I would you had liv'd so, my Lord that I,
   Might rather have continu'd your poore servant,
   Then sit here as your Judge.
DU CROYE.   I am sorry for you.   155
ROCHFORT.   In no act of my life I have deserv'd
   This injury from the court, that any heere
   Should thus uncivilly usurpe on what
   Is proper to me only.
DU CROYE.   What distaste   160
   Receives my Lord?
ROCHFORT.   You say you are sorry for him:
   A griefe in which I must not have a partner:
   'Tis I alone am sorry, that I rays'd
   The building of my life for seventy yeeres   165
   Upon so sure a ground, that all the vices
   Practis'd to ruine man, though brought against me,
   Could never undermine, and no way left
   To send these gray haires to the grave with sorrow.
   Vertue that was my patronesse, betrayd me: 170
   For entring, nay, possessing this young man,
   It lent him such a powerfull Majesty
   To grace what ere he undertooke, that freely
   I gave my selfe up with my liberty,
   To be at his disposing; had his person,   175
   Lovely I must confesse, or far fam'd valour,
   Or any other seeming good, that yet
   Holds a neere neyghbour-hood, with ill wrought on me,
   I might have borne it better: but when goodnesse
   And piety it selfe in her best figure   180
   Were brib'd to my destruction, can you blame me,
   Though I forget to suffer like a man,
   Or rather act a woman?
BEAUMONT.   Good my Lord.
NOVALL SENIOR.   You hinder our proceeding.   185
CHARMI.   And forget
   The parts of an accuser.

BEAUMONT.   Pray you remember
To use the temper which to me you promis'd.
ROCHFORT.   Angels themselves must breake *Baumont*, that
   promise   190
   Beyond the strength and patience of Angels.
   But I have done, my good Lord, pardon me
   A weake old man, and pray adde to that
   A miserable father, yet be carefull
   That your compassion of my age, nor his,   195
   Move you to any thing, that may dis-become
   The place on which you sit.
CHARMI.   Read the Inditement.
CHARALOIS.   It shall be needelesse, I my selfe, my Lords,
   Will be my owne accuser, and confesse   200
   All they can charge me with, nor will I spare
   To aggravate that guilt with circumstance
   They seeke to loade me with: onely I pray,
   That as for them you will vouchsafe me hearing:
   I may not be denide it for my selfe,   205
   When I shall urge by what unanswerable reasons
   I was compel'd to what I did, which yet
   Till you have taught me better, I repent not.
ROCHFORT.   The motion honest.
CHARMI.   And 'tis freely granted.   210
CHARALOIS.   Then I confesse my Lords, that I stood bound,
   When with my friends, even hope it selfe had left me
   To this mans charity for my liberty,
   Nor did his bounty end there, but began:
   For after my enlargment, cherishing   215
   The good he did, he made me master of
   His onely daughter, and his whole estate:
   Great ties of thankfulnesse I must acknowledge,
   Could any one fee'd by you, presse this further?
   But yet consider, my most honour'd Lords,   220
   If to receive a favour, make a servant,
   And benefits are bonds to tie the taker
   To the imperious will of him that gives,
   Ther's none but slaves will receive courtesie,

               219 fee'd] freed Q.

Since they must fetter us to our dishonours.   225
Can it be cal'd magnificence in a Prince,
To powre downe riches, with a liberall hand,
Upon a poore mans wants, if that must bind him
To play the soothing parasite to his vices?
Or any man, because he sav'd my hand,   230
Presume my head and heart are at his service?
Or did I stand ingag'd to buy my freedome
(When my captivity was honourable)
By making my selfe here and fame hereafter,
Bondslaves to mens scorne and calumnious tongues?   235
Had his faire daughters mind bin like her feature,
Or for some little blemish I had sought
For my content elsewhere, wasting on others
My body and her dowry; my forhead then
Deserv'd the brand of base ingratitude: 240
But if obsequious usage, and faire warning
To keepe her worth my love, could not preserve her
From being a whore, and yet no cunning one,
So to offend and yet the fault kept from me?
What should I doe? let any freeborne spirit   245
Determine truly, if that thankfulnesse,
Choise forme with the whole world given for a dowry,
Could strengthen so an honest man with patience,
As with a willing necke to undergoe
The insupportable yoake of slave or wittoll.   250
CHARMI.   What proofe have you she did play false, besides
Your oath?
CHARALOIS.   Her owne confession to her father.
I aske him for a witnesse.
ROCHFORT.   'Tis most true.   255
I would not willingly blend my last words
With an untruth.
CHARALOIS.   And then to cleere my selfe,
That his great wealth was not the marke I shot at,
But that I held it, when faire *Beaumelle*   260
Fell from her vertue, like the fatall gold
Which *Brennus* tooke from *Delphos*, whose possession
Brought with it ruine to himselfe and Army.

F.D.—4*

Heer's one in Court, *Baumont*, by whom I sent
All graunts and writings backe, which made it mine,   265
Before his daughter dy'd by his owne sentence,
As freely as unask'd he gave it to me.
BEAUMONT.   They are here to be seene.
CHARALOIS.   Open the casket.
Peruse that deed of gift.   270
ROMONT.   Halfe of the danger
Already is discharg'd: the other part
As bravely, and you are not onely free,
But crownd with praise for ever.
DU CROYE.   'Tis apparent.   275
CHARMI.   Your state, my Lord, againe is yours.
ROCHFORT.   Not mine,
I am not of the world, if it can prosper,
(And yet being justly got, Ile not examine
Why it should be so fatall) doe you bestow it   280
On pious uses. Ile goe seeke a grave.
And yet for proofe, I die in peace, your pardon
I aske, and as you grant it me, may Heaven
Your conscience, and these Judges free you from
What you are charg'd with. So farewell for ever—   285

Exit ROCHFORT.

NOVALL SENIOR.   Ile be mine owne guide. Passion, not
example
Shall be my leaders. I have lost a sonne,
A sonne, grave Judges, I require his blood
From his accursed homicide.
CHARMI.   What reply you   290
In your defence for this?
CHARALOIS.   I but attended
Your Lordships pleasure. For the fact, as of
The former, I confesse it, but with what
Base wrongs I was unwillingly drawne to it,   295
To my few words there are some other proofes
To witnesse this for truth, when I was married:
For there I must begin. The slayne *Novall*
Was to my wife, in way of our French courtship,

A most devoted servant, but yet aym'd at   300
Nothing but meanes to quench his wanton heate,
His heart being never warm'd by lawfull fires
As mine was (Lords:) and though on these presumptions,
Joyn'd to the hate betweene his house and mine,
I might with opportunity and ease   305
Have found a way for my revenge, I did not;
But still he had the freedome as before
When all was mine, and told that he abus'd it
With some unseemely licence, by my friend
My approv'd friend *Romont*, I gave no credit   310
To the reporter, but reprov'd him for it,
As one uncourtly and malicious to him.
What could I more, my Lords? yet after this
He did continue in his first pursute
Hoter then ever, and at length obtain it;   315
But how it came to my most certaine knowledge,
For the dignity of the court and my owne honour
I dare not say.
NOVALL SENIOR.   If all may be beleev'd
A passionate prisoner speakes, who is so foolish   320
That durst be wicked, that will appeare guilty?
No, my grave Lords: in his impunity
But give example unto jealous men
To cut the throats they hate, and they will never
Want matter or pretence for their bad ends.   325
CHARMI.   You must finde other proofes to strengthen these
But meere presumptions.
DU CROYE.   Or we shall hardly
Allow your innocence.
CHARALOIS.   All your attempts   330
Shall fall on me, like brittle shafts on armor,
That breake themselves; or like waves against a rocke,
That leave no signe of their ridiculous fury
But foame and splinters, my innocence like these
Shall stand triumphant, and your malice serve   335
But for a trumpet to proclaime my conquest;
Nor shall you, though you doe the worst fate can,
How ere condemne, affright an honest man.

ROMONT.   May it please the Court, I may be heard.
NOVALL SENIOR.   You come not   340
  To raile againe? but doe, you shall not finde
  Another *Rochfort*.
ROMONT.   In *Novall* I cannot.
  But I come furnished with what will stop
  The mouth of his conspiracy against the life   345
  Of innocent *Charaloys*. Doe you know this Character?
NOVALL SENIOR.   Yes, 'tis my sonnes.
ROMONT.   May it please your Lordships, reade it,
  And you shall finde there, with what vehemency
  He did sollicite *Beaumelle*, how he had got   350
  A promise from her to injoy his wishes,
  How after he abjur'd her company,
  And yet, but that 'tis fit I spare the dead,
  Like a damnd villaine, assoone as recorded,
  He brake that oath, to make this manifest   355
  Produce his bauds and hers.

Enter AYMER, FLORIMELL, BELLAPERT.

CHARMI.   Have they tooke their oathes?
ROMONT.   They have; and rather then indure the racke,
  Confesse the time, the meeting, nay the act;
  What would you more? onely this matron made   360
  A free discovery to a good end;
  And therefore I sue to the Court, she may not
  Be plac'd in the blacke list of the delinquents.
PONTALIER.   I see by this, *Novals* revenge needs me,
  And I shall doe.   365
CHARMI.   'Tis evident.
NOVALL SENIOR.   That I
  Till now was never wretched, here's no place
  To curse him or my stars.

                              Exit NOVALL SENIOR.

CHARMI.   Lord *Charalois*,   370
  The injuries you have sustain'd, appeare
                    356 bauds] bands Q.

So worthy of the mercy of the Court,
That notwithstanding you have gone beyond
The letter of the Law, they yet acquit you.
PONTALIER.   But in *Novall*, I doe condemne him thus.   375

                    ⟨*Stabs Charalois.*⟩

CHARALOIS.   I am slayne.
ROMONT.   Can I looke on? Oh murderous wretch,
Thy challenge now I answere. So die with him.

                    ⟨*Stabs Pontalier.*⟩

CHARMI.   A guard: disarme him.
ROMONT.   I yeeld up my sword   380
Unforc'd. Oh *Charaloys*.
CHARALOIS.   For shame, *Romont*,
Mourne not for him that dies as he hath liv'd,
Still constant and unmov'd: what's falne upon me,
Is by Heavens will, because I made my selfe   385
A Judge in my owne cause without their warrant:
But he that lets me know thus much in death,
With all good men forgive mee.
PONTALIER.   I receive the vengeance, which my love
Not built on vertue, has made me worthy, worthy of.   390
CHARMI.   We are taught
By this sad president, how just soever
Our reasons are to remedy our wrongs,
We are yet to leave them to their will and power,
That to that purpose have authority.   395
For you, *Romont*, although in your excuse
You may plead, what you did, was in revenge
Of the dishonour done unto the Court:
Yet since from us you had not warrant for it,
We banish you the State: for these, they shall,
As they are found guilty, or innocent,
Be set free, or suffer punishment.   402

                    Exeunt omnes

FINIS.

TEXTUAL NOTES

SIGLA

Q = Quarto, 1632.
Qc = Corrected Quarto: reading drawn from another copy collated with copy-text.
G = Gifford's Second Edition (1813).
L = Lockert's Edition (1918).
M = Monck Mason's Edition (1779).

The caret mark ʌ is used throughout the Notes to indicate the absence of punctuation; the wavy dash ∼ denotes the exact repetition of a word given in the lemma.

I. I

44	him? ∼. Q.
70	No,] ∼ʌ Q.
101	borne ever] ∼, ∼ Q.
116	goodnesse.] ∼? Q.
129	adde.] ∼ʌ Q.
183	That] that Q.
203	on;] ∼, Q.
207	s.d. CREDITORS] Creditor Q.

I. II

Scene-heading om. by Q.
CREDITORS] *Presidents* Q.

1	Prosperous] prosperous Q.
23	mention.] ∼, Q.
27	yeeres!] ∼. Q.
69	With, ... that,] ∼ʌ ... ∼ʌ Q.
75	remember.] ∼, Q.
129	wear'st] wear.st Q.
167	counsayle, were it a] ∼ʌ ∼ ∼, ∼ Q.
211	from] frõ Q.
214	warre.] ∼, Q.
273	tongue] tougue Q.
274	revenge] renenge Q.
278	answer] auswer Q.

II. I

4	judgement] *m* is upside-down in Q.
7	free-living] free living Q.
50	s.d. *Mourners, Scutchions, etc., very*] *Mourners. Scutchions, and very* Q.
89	perfume.] ∼ʌ Q.
107	yee] shee Q.
147	you heare] Q; you are heare L.
154	were i'the Burmudas.] were the Burmudas. Q.
155	JAYLOR] *Saylor* Q.

II. II

5	to] To Q.
11	women!] ∼? Q.
17	served] serue Q.
37	Ud's-light] Ud'd-light Q.
80	discipline) falne] ∼ʌ ∼) Q.
107	lie] liue Q.
114	Mistress] Mrs Q.
125	drover.] ∼, Q.
136	Mistress.] Mrs Q.
138	Mistress'] Mrs Q.

148   consume.] ~, Q.
162   s.d. *to* BEAUMELLE.)] — to his
      M^rs Q (printed as text).
163   s.d.   ROCHFORT,   BEAU-
      MELLE.] *Roch.Daug.* Q.
174   feares] teares Q.
175   s.d. BEAUMELLE.] *Daug.* Q.
175   s.d. ROMONT, KEEPER.]
      Romont keeper. Q.
187   opportunity] Q; M, followed by
      later editors, emended to "op-
      portunely". This emendation is
      probably correct. Conservative
      principles, however, suggest that
      Q's reading, to which reasonable
      sense adheres, should stand.
203   strong-breath'd] strong breath Q.
230   soul-lesse] L says his copy
      prints "lsoul-esse".
245   it tends.] is tends? Q.
245   s.d. BEAUMONT] *Seruant* Q.
294   mocke !] ~? Q.
305   *Charolois,*] ~. Q.
314   an asse. Pay] ana sse_ʌ Pay Q.
319   blushes scald] bushes, cal'd Q.
320   offer] offter Q.
321   you,] ~. Q.
325   appeares] ~, Q.
326   see,] ~_ʌ Q.
326   education] ~, Q.
337   participate] Q. Edd. have emended
      to "precipitate" here.
340   vertue,] ~_ʌ Q.
344   vanisht.] ~_ʌ Q.
356   This line is assigned only to
      Beau. in Q. Though Beaumont
      appears more often as *Bau.*, it
      seems more natural that this
      should be his speech.
382   LILADAM. *Aymer,* here] *Lilad.
      Aym.* Here Q. Q appears to
      assign this line to both Liladam
      and Aymer. Possibly each should
      take one of the sentences as they
      go off. More probably, as
      rendered here, the line should go
      to Liladam alone.

III. I

15   could_ʌ] ~. Q.
24   will —] will_ʌ Q.
56   onely:] ~_ʌ Q.
57   Rivall?] ~. Q.
60   With next gold] Q; L prints
      "With the next gold".
70   now] know Q.
84   his liking] this likening Q.
      Probably the ms spelling was
      "likeing". (Edd. have also
      emended "reverence" to "re-
      ference", but this is unjustified.)
120   suddainly] suddaily Q.
135   yee] This word is illegible in Q
      and all edd. supply "thee".
137   sillable] Q syllable L.
141   entertainment] entertaiment Q.
148   Lady?] ~. Q.
206   counsayle_ʌ] ~. Q.
223   entertainmment] Q; entertain-
      ment L.
269   inclin'd — to] inclin'd to Q.
276   ha!] ~? Q.
298   kissing!] ~? Q.
318   *Romont* —] ~. Q.
320   Reprov'd] Reproue Q.
426   defect] detect Q.
468   should] ~_ʌ Q.
477   *Lockes*] *Locke* Q.
479   your strength] you ~ Q.
494   your] yonr Q.
542   thy] my Q.
553   thinke).] ~.) Q.

IV. I

7   Lord!] ~, Q.
27–8 loome as nature fram'd his
      Lordship,] ~, ~ ... ~_ʌ Q.
37   mistres] misters Q.
43   otherwise] Qc; othewrise Q.
62   admirable lecture!] admirable!
      lecture. Q.
66   Flatters —] ~, Q.
89   for!] ~? Q.
106   honour_ʌ] ~. Q.

124 challenge:] ~, Q.
124 fate‸] ~: Q.
148 a] A Q.

IV. II

10   something else,] ~, ~ Q.
34   let] ler Q.
66   servants] sernants Q.
71   rare —] ~, Q.
95   towne] Q; town L.
105 murther,] murrher, Q.
127 whores daring,] ~, ~ Q.
131 flesh.] ~‸ Q.

IV. IV

38   inhabit;] ~, Q.
42   practise,] ~‸ Q.
43   shame;] ~: Q.
44   securely:] ~, Q.
64   was,] ~‸ Q.
148 his] L (without note), G; this Q.
152 one] owne Q.
162 live:] ~‸ Q.
164 one] on Q.
165 fervour] fervuor Q.
182 doome.] ~‸ Q.

V. I

36   and thefe] are these Q.
80   abject] obiect Q.
83   Away!] ~‸ Q.
85   Captaine?] ~. Q.
120 one] ones Q.
121 Addition] Additions Q.

V. II

26   grievd] grieue Q.
32   have,] ~‸ Q.
37   Scythian] Q; Sythian L. (His
     repetition of this spelling in his
     note suggests strongly that he
     renders his copy-text accurately.)
44   worthy] worrhy Q.
66   cause? *Romont*!] cause Romont?
     Q.
84   man —] ~‸ Q.
107 chalenged] chalenge Q.
111 tombe.] ~‸ Q.
176 fam'd] fain'd Q.
181 my] Q; by L (supported by his
     note). Clearly he had an uncor-
     rected sheet in his copy-text.
     (He also reads "accnser" at 1.200
     and "coufesse" at 1.211.)
189 promis'd] ~; Q.
197 sit.] ~‸ Q.
201 nor] or Q.
242 could not preserve] could pre-
     serue Q.
252 Your] your Q.
269 CHARALOIS.] *Charmi.* Q.
     Clearly the compositor has mis-
     taken the abbreviated assign-
     ment (probably "*Char.*") here
     and given this speech to Charmi
     (erring also in the catchword on
     L2ᵛ) when clearly it must belong
     to Charalois.
286 not] nor Q.
310 approv'd] appou'd Q.
316 knowledge] kowledge Q.

COMMENTARY

I. I

18 Noble] Rather a weak joke. Romont hands Charmi, as his fee, a coin ("noble"), thus "ennobling" him.

59–62 Rochfort and Du Croye are greeting Charalois, who does not answer them.

70 ribons] ribbons worn to indicate mourning.

71 had no eyes, To see] refused to recognise.

85 to her succours] to the help she (justice) can give.

121 At this point Charalois offers his petition.

134 heare] *i.e.* listen to.

166–7 Romont means that it depends on how the matter is brought to Novall's attention. He then turns to Liladam, and presumably takes hold of him, when he is cut short by Novall's exit.

167 s.d. ADVOCATES] Thus Q, although they have not been marked as entering.

175 ensignes] *i.e.* signs. Liladam is indicating his attire.

203 hornes] Romont has already called them cuckolds (1.197).

I. II

36 affection ... but] inclination ... except.

104 place you plead at] *i.e.* the bar. Novall means that Charmi will appear behind the bar, at which prisoners stand.

125 purple-colour'd] Judges wore purple on occasion.

143 subtill Fox of France] Louis XI of France.

193 The warlike *Charloyes*] Charles the Bold, Duke of Burgundy, defeated at Granson (1476), Morat (1476), and Nancy (1477) by the Swiss.

217 good] *i.e.* good in credit, financially sound.

274 that way of revenge] *i.e.* by using his tongue.

304 it] *i.e.* the place.

326 it skills not] it matters not.

II. I

13–14 To let strong nature . . .] To let natural inclinations (*i.e.* emotions) have the upper hand in such a case over all tendencies towards reason (or perhaps, all that reason to which he lays claim).

49 interd] *i.e.* enter'd.

86 The golden calfe] *i.e.* the proud, rich man.

88 consume] *i.e.* be consumed.

107 with a birth] from the same cause.

137 My roote] *i.e.* his father.

141 This] Here he holds his father's sword.

145 s.d. It is not clear who sings this song — presumably one of the musicians.

152 At this point the procession is about to move on.

159 dogs in July] By a confusion, rabies was thought to be commonest during the "dog-days", though this hot season is so called because the Dog-star rises then.

II. II

16   hood] The hood is the symbol of the rank one assumes.

18   peepe out] *i.e.* pip out. Not quite the thing; a reference to the card-game of one-and-thirty.

40   servant] *i.e.* devoted follower. This word is used in this sense throughout the play.

85   under a weede] in clothes; a phrase used for all womanhood.

91   a three-leg'd Lord] like a joint-stool, something manufactured.

101   Gally-slops] Q prints "Gally-foyst", which is the Lord Mayor's barge. This makes no sense in context. "Bullion" (1.102) was an elaborate type of hose; "Quirpo", a variant of Sp. "cuerpo", means "undress". Liladam appears in clothes inappropriate to the time of day, since Novall hangs his clothes upon him as a "dressing blocke" before donning them himself. "Gally-slops" were a kind of wide hose, and this emendation gives the passage the required third type of dress, as well as being palaeographically acceptable.

106   cast skins] cast-off clothes.

123   St. *Omers*] St. Omer, where there was a College of Jesuits: an allusion here to Jesuit spies coming across to England on some pretext.

126   ly'n perdieu] "to lie perdieu" means to be on sentry-duty.

130   tye my hand] lit., tie the ribbons at her cuff. At this point Beaumelle holds out her hand and Novall kisses it, possibly after tying the ribbon. At her encouragement, he moves on to kiss her lips.

136–48   Though assigned to Aymer by Novall, this song might be sung by Aymer and Bellapert, since it is a dialogue. It certainly should not be sung by Novall and Beaumelle as suggested by .Q

175   s.D. KEEPER] Presumably the same "Jaylor" as in II. I. 155.

210   eager relish] sharp taste.

265   How silken is this well] In default of any satisfactory emendation for "well" this must be accepted as an inappropriate metaphor. Presumably the "well" refers to Charalois' tears and the "silken" to the terms in which he expresses his grief.

282   tender] *i.e.* to tender, offer.

285–87   The opposition here is between the spirited and passionate ("high-blouded veines")and virtue.

326–7   her education Followes not any) her education is second to none.

339   in which yours] since she is yours.

365   The punctuation of this line indicates the pauses in which he is kissing Beaumelle.

372   *Curtius*-like] Marcus Curtius, legendary hero of Rome, who sacrificed himself for his country by leaping on horseback into a chasm which had opened in the Forum.

380   vane] *i.e.* weather-vane.

405   s.D. the Act] The interval between the Acts, while music is being played.

III. I

13   that pleasure] *i.e.* which Charalois has enjoyed (1.7) in marrying Beaumelle.

34   take me with you] you follow what I mean.

38   gamesters] those who play the "game" (in a special sense).

44   Bellapert speaks this line sarcastically.

53   one] *i.e.* maidenhead.

102   my fellow] *i.e.* Bellapert.

137   On] *i.e.* one.

139   Christian] human being.

141-2   Editors have tried to make sense of these lines by suggesting that "on" is an old spelling for "one". Romont is saying, "The way in which you have been received here (by Beaumelle) has made what I intended on into a serious matter." Possibly "on" is a misprint for "of".

144   legge] a bow.

146   Muske-cat] civet-cat; an opprobrious term for a scented fop.

148   charges] *i.e.* expense (in buying perfume). Beaumelle then turns this upon Romont by suggesting, in a "nasty scoffe" that perfume is necessary now he has come.

202   in spite of] in contempt of.

221   cast suburbe whores] Brothels were commonly outside the walls, since they were not, officially, tolerated within the city-limits. Here prostitutes were more numerous, and of lower quality, than within the city. To be cast off from such service and relegated to "the Campe" indicates the status of such women.

225   Legion] of devils.

226   horne-mad] raving with anger, with the additional sense, picked up in this line, of being angry at being cuckolded.

227   come to] attained, that is, in Charalois' service.

230-1   use, The liberty that best likes me] do as I please.

235   yellow] with jealousy.

245   carted] Dragging through the town on a cart, or sometimes whipping at the cart-tail, was the common penalty for prostitution.

295   perfect] *i.e.* in your part, a theatrical term.

346   I] Here this could possibly, but not certainly, mean "Aye".

506-7   flegme ... choller] the two "humours" in the Elizabethan physiology responsible for, respectively, apathy and irascibility.

549   mens marginall fingers] The typographic device of a pointing hand ("fist") was frequently used to draw attention to an important passage in a book. *Cf.* IV. I. 52.

IV. I

3   red-headed woman] In traditional superstition (which prevails to this day), red-headed women have a powerful sexual odour.

24-5   M. Channing Linthicum, in her *Costume in the Drama of Shakespeare and his Contemporaries* (New York, 1936, reissued 1963) p. 164, thinks that this passage refers to the likelihood of Novall's barber damaging his clothes should he make "a haire breadth's error"! Liladam, of course, is referring to the precise cut of the clothes — and with a professional eye, as we discover in v. I.

36   I] *i.e.* Aye.

70   natures copy ... forme] A metaphor from printing.

92   Barber Surgeon] Barbers were also surgeons and dentists.

120   Sent] *i.e.* scent.

129   close breeches] Tight-fitting trousers. Romont, as a soldier, wore these.

136   under a Lord] with anyone under the rank of Lord.

141   *Colbran*] Colbrand, the wicked giant in the tale of Guy of Warwick.

146   Consort] itinerant musician, wont to thrust himself uninvited into company with the phrase "By your leave".

214–5 Fairies treasure] Superstition held that to reveal the source of a gift given by a fairy caused it to vanish.

IV. II

36 Aymer is speaking to someone outside as he comes in.

55 consent] From Aymer's next speech it seems this is the correct reading, not "content" (*i.e.* "contend"), as editors have suggested. Charalois means he doesn't agree with Aymer, not that he will not allow him to keep the musicians concealed.

58 *Song above.*] This song is sung from the gallery above the stage, whereas the second song is sung from the stage itself or from below the stage.

76 well of] far away.

97 groome] *i.e.* bridegroom, husband.

110 on all advantage] taking every advantage of you.

125 bloods wrongs] wrongs done to kindred.

129 in her quarrell] on her behalf.

143 forthcoming] be available when the matter is investigated.

IV. III

21 except against] take exception against: but, more probably, "accept" may be meant.

IV. IV

8 Beaumelle is kneeling before him.
93 Mole] *i.e.* blind.

V. I

4 Liladam's name has been joined to Novall's in the contract with the tailor.

14 coming forth] appearance in court. *Cf.* note on IV. II. 143.

20 two supporters] *i.e.* the officers.

27–32 There is a complex play on words here, which previous editors have struggled with unsuccessfully. Yet it may be understood generally, if not precisely. The "ten crowne supper for cloth of bodkin" is the making of a suit out of expensive cloth — which, of course, the tailor has not paid for. He is partaking of this feast along with the Gallants and, in the process, can, unobserved, purloin enough material for "three manchets". A "manchette" was an elaborate cuff, and it may be conjectured that a "Larke" is a now-lost descriptive name for a style of dress (perhaps a cloak), or possibly some technical term in tailoring. The gastronomic figure is possible because "manchet" is also a small loaf of fine, white flour.

34 hanger] short sword, used by the officers. "Leave" in this line is not a verb but an adjective, and might be a misprint for "leane" (*i.e.* penniless). "Hangers" (1.97) refers to the sword-belt.

5 next way] *i.e.* to undo himself. "Next" means "nearest".

49 action entred] entered before the Court. Properly speaking, no arrest could be made without legal proceedings.

82 basket] the Sheriff's basket. The left-overs from the Sheriff's household were put in a basket and fed to penniless prisoners. *Cf. City Madam*, I. I. 146.

97 Hell] the space under a tailor's bench, into which scraps of cloth were thrown, to become the tailor's perquisites.

102 buttred loaves] Traditionally, tailors were great eaters of bread.

104 use a conscience] be tender-
hearted.
105 hall] the hall of the guild of
tailors, hence the trade-guild itself.
112 compleate Mounsieur] perfect
gentleman.
120–1 one Addition] Liladam is
referring to the cod-piece.
122 worke out] *i.e.* pay for by work-
ing.

V. II

36 heires] *i.e.* hairs.
52 hornes] a derisory gesture, im-

puting cuckoldry, still common in
Italy.
53 they] *i.e.* horns.
121 by pieces] in part.
262 *Brennus*] a leader of Gaul who
attacked Greece in the second
century B.C. He did not, in fact,
sack Delphi, unlike a predecessor,
another Brennus, who in 390 B.C.
attacked Rome and left with a large
ransom in gold. The two have become confused in this passage.
278 can prosper] can bring any good.
320 speakes] *i.e.* says.
360 this matron] presumably Florimell.

BIBLIOGRAPHY

ABBREVIATIONS

M.L.N. = *Modern Language Notes*
M.L.R. = *Modern Language Review*
N.&Q. = *Notes and Queries*
P.M.L.A. = *Publications of the Modern Language Association*
S.B. = *Studies in Bibliography*

I. WORKS OF MASSINGER AND FIELD

A. COLLECTED AND SELECTED EDITIONS

1. *Massinger*

The Dramatic Works of Philip Massinger, ed. T. Coxeter, 4 vols. London 1761.

The Dramatick Works of Philip Massinger, ed. J. Monck Mason, 4 vols. London 1779.

The Plays of Philip Massinger, ed. W. Gifford, 4 vols, Second Edition. London 1813.

The Dramatic Works of Massinger and Ford, ed. H. Coleridge. London 1839–40.

The Plays of Philip Massinger, ed. F. Cunningham. London 1871.

The Best Plays of the Old Dramatists: Philip Massinger, ed. A. Symons, 2 vols, Mermaid Series. London 1887–89. (A Selection, including *The Fatal Dowry*.)

2. *Field*

The Plays of Nathan Field, ed. W. Peery. Austin (U. of Texas P.) 1950.

A. *THE FATAL DOWRY*

The Fatall Dowry: A Tragedy . . . by P.M. and N.F.: First Quarto, 1632.

The Fatal Dowry, ed. C. L. Lockert: Lancaster, Pa. (New Era) 1918.

II. STUDIES BY OTHERS

A. GENERAL

1. *Textual*

CHELLI, MAURICE. *Étude sur la Collaboration de Massinger avec Fletcher et son Groupe.* Paris (Presses Universitaires) 1926.

HOY, CYRUS. "The Shares of Fletcher and his Collaborators in the Beaumont and Fletcher Canon", in *S.B.* VIII–IX, XI–XV (1955–62).

2. Critical

BRINKLEY, R. F. "Nathan and Nathaniel Field", in *M.L.N.*, XLII (1927), pp. 10–15.

——. *Nathan Field, the Actor Playwright*: New Haven (Yale U. P.) 1928.

CHELLI, MAURICE. *Le Drame de Massinger*: Lyons (M. Audin) 1923.

CRUICKSHANK, A. H. *Philip Massinger*: Oxford (Oxford U.P.) 1920.

DUNN, T. A. *Philip Massinger: The Man and the Playwright*: London (Nelson) 1957.

ELIOT, T. S. "Philip Massinger", in *The Sacred Wood*. London (Faber) 1920. Reprinted in *Selected Essays*. London (Faber) 1932.

PEERY, W. "Field's Dates", in *M.L.R.*, XLI (1946), p. 409.

VERHASSELT, E. "A Biography of Field, Dramatist and Actor", in *Revue belge*, XXV (1947), pp. 00–00.

B. THE FATAL DOWRY
1. Critical

LOCKERT, C. L. "A Scene in *The Fatal Dowry*", in *M.L.N.*, XXV (1920), pp. 291–3.

WAITH, E. M. "*Cont-oversia* in the English Drama: Medwall and Massinger", in *P.M.L.A.*, LXVIII (1953), pp. 286–303.

2. Stage History

KERMODE, J. F. "A Note on the History of *The Fatal Dowry* in the Eighteenth Century", in *N.&Q.*, 3 May 1947.

ROWE, NICHOLAS. *Three Plays ... by Nicholas Rowe*, ed. J. R. Sutherland. London (Scholartis Press) 1929.

[SCOTT, SIR WALTER]. "A Comparison of *The Fatal Dowry* with *The Fair Penitent*", in *Observer* lxxvii–lxxix. Reprinted in Giford's edition, vol. III, pp. 466–85.

GLOSSARY

abjur'd	*renounced*, V. II. 352.
admit	*allow, permit*, III. I. 547.
alone	*only*, III. I. 39, 167.
bale	*bail*, II. I. 61.
band	*ruff, collar*, II. II. 79, 113, IV. I. 166.
bankerupt	*bankrupt*, II. II. 300.
banquerout	*bankrupt*, I. I. 154, I. II. 100.
banquet	*dessert, light refreshments*, IV. II. 37.
basket	*Sheriff's basket (See* Commentary), V. I. 82.
beaver	*hat*, V. I. 98.
bile	*boil*, II. II. 198.
blemish	*fault*, V. II. 237.
bodkin, cloth of	*a rich brocade (from Fr.* Baudekin, *It.* Baldacco = *Bagdad*), V. I. 30.
boord	*boarding, lodging*, IV. I. 40.
bullion	*elaborate trunk-hose, puffed out at the top*, II. II. 102.
bumfiddles	*beats*, IV. I. 149.
calenture	*a tropical fever*, III. I. 461.
cap a pe	*cap a pied, head to foot*, III. I. 201.
caparisons	*trappings (of a horse)*, II. II. 200.
cape (*i.e.* cappe)	*cap*, V. I. 99.
caroch, caroch	*coach*, II. 28, IV. II. 138.
carriage	*behaviour, deportment*, II. II. 182.
case	*disguise*, V. I. 86.
cause	*case (legal)*, I. I. 9, 12, 27; *affair*, III. I. 437, 448.
censure	*judgment*, I. II. 62; *sentence*, II. II. 195.
ceremonious	*punctilious*, I. II. 189.
character	*handwriting*, V. II. 346.
cheapen	*bargain*, IV. II. 87.
cholericke	*hot-tempered*, II. I. 112.
close	*close-fitting*, IV. I. 129.
clout	*cloth*, II. II. 127.
commission, gives	*allows, permits*, III. I. 128.
confirm'd	*established*, I. II. 285.
conscious	*having guilty knowledge*, III. I. 421.
considerate	*careful*, I. II. 253.
constraine	*insist, compel, force*, II. II. 232.
contemn'd	*disregarded, scornfully refused*, I. I. 124.
cooze	*friend*, IV. I. 130.

courtesie, courtesy *favour, kindness,* II. II. 370, III. I. 33, 35, 38, 41; *generous treatment,* V. II. 224.

courtship *the code of good manners (particularly of the fashionable sort),* III. I. 324, 521, V. II. 299.

credits *reputations,* I. II. 77.

curace *cuirass, breast-plate,* II. I. 127.

curious *careful,* IV. I. 106; *delicate, dainty,* IV. II. 63.

curiosity *elaborate care (of construction),* hence, *rarity,* II. II. 69.

curryer *one who dresses and tans leather,* III. I. 396.

dag *pistol,* IV. I. 180 S.D.

danger *power, mercy;* hence, *debt,* I. II. 232, V. II. 271. (*Cf.* City Madam, v. II. 84, 85.)

defeatures *defeats,* I. II. 200.

designe *plot,* IV. IV. 205.

determine *pass sentence on,* II. II. 196.

detract *disparage,* I. II. 306.

dighted *arrayed, dressed,* IV. I. 46.

discover *reveal,* III. I. 285, IV. II. 100.

discovery *disclosure,* III. I. 104; *revelation,* V. II. 361.

disputed *argued,* I. II. 292.

distance, in *within striking distance,* III. I. 306.

doome *iudgment,* IV. IV. 182.

doubtfull *fearful, frightened,* IV. II. 129.

dramme *the smallest weight,* III. I. 519.

earth'd *buried,* II. I. 137.

edify *gain instruction, learn,* IV. I. 58.

electuary *a medicine, compounded out of a bitter with a sweet coating,* II. II. 10.

elements *the four elements, earth, air, fire, water,* I. II. 165.

engender *mingle (lit. copulate),* III. I. 501.

engine *plot, device,* III. I. 183.

enlargement *order for release,* I. II. 313; *freeing from prison,* V. II. 215.

entertainment *pay, allowance,* I. II. 211.

Ephimerides *table showing the position of a heavenly body day by day,* IV. I. 30.

ernest *advance on money owed,* V. I. 51.

except at *take exception to,* III. I. 173.

execution *writ of execution (to carry out a court order),* I. II. 280.

exhaust *draw out, produce,* II. I. 111.

factor *agent,* I. II. 156.

feares *is afraid for,* IV. II. 131.

fee'd *hired for a fee (as a lawyer),* V. II. 219.

fit *punish appropriately,* III. I. 296.

flaxe *wick,* IV. I. 3.

forespake	*predicted,* III. I. 294.
free	*frank, open,* V. II. 361.
freedome	*liberty to speak freely, privilege,* I. I. 66.
gallimaufry	*medley, jumble, mixture,* II. II. 97.
gally-slops	*loose, wide hose, gallygaskins,* II. II. 101.
gigglet	*light, frivolous woman,* III. I. 362.
gowneman	*lawyer,* I. II. 146.
grav'd	*buried,* III. I. 548.
gull	*deceive,* III. I. 259.
habit	*dress,* I. I. 69.
hand	*signature,* IV. I. 207, 208.
hanger	*short sword,* V. I. 34.
hangers	*ornate sword-belt,* V. I. 97.
hire	*bribe,* I. I. 104.
hoboyes	*oboes,* II. II. 405 S.D.
homely	*homily,* III. I. 215.
homicide	*murderer,* V. II. 289.
horslocke	*shackle (for horse's feet),* IV. I. 75.
impertinence	*irrelevance,* I. II. 74.
impudence	*shamelessness,* III. I. 248.
intestine	*internal,* V. II. 122.
Jacob's staffe	*astrolabe, for measuring sun's altitude,* IV. I. 30.
jealous	*suspicious,* III. I. 414.
jennet	*small horse,* IV. I. 77.
lacquay	*lackey, running-footman,* IV. I. 117.
lawlesse	*without respect for the law,* I. I. 182.
league	*leaguer, military-camp,* III. I. 204.
lists	*strips (of cloth),* V. I. 99.
lively	*living,* II. I. 49; *lifelike,* II. II. 260.
lower	*shorter,* II. II. 96.
luxury	*lechery, extravagance,* I. I. 201.
mainely	*entirely,* II. I. 140.
manchets	(a) *ornamental cuffs (manchettes);* (b) *small loaves of fine white flour,* V. I. 31.
modell	*design, cut,* IV. I. 10.
mome	*fool,* IV. II. 93.
moyety	*half,* I. II. 315.
murrion	*murrain, plague,* III. I. 301.
nice	*wanton,* III. I. 524.
noble	*a gold coin (usually worth 6s 8d),* I. I. 18.

obnoxious — *liable (to attack)*, III. I. 422.
observers — *obsequious followers*, IV. IV. 46.
overthrowne — *thrown too far*, IV. I. 98.

pantofle — *slipper (hence, applied here to the trade of shoe-making)*, V. I. 117.
parciall — *partial*, II. I. 38.
parts — *job*, I. I. 11.
passage — *procession*, II. II. 405 S.D.
per se — *intrinsically, essentially*, II. II. 84.
pickadille — *stiffened support for a broad collar*, IV. I. 25.
pointed — *be-ribboned*, III. I. 185.
policy — *scheming*, IV. IV. 212.
pown'd — *confined*, IV. I. 81.
practise — *perform, put into execution*, I. I. 120; *deceit*, IV. IV. 42.
præcipuce (*i.e.* precipice) — *fall*, III. I. 546.
præter — *except*, I. II. 329 S.D., II. II. 163 S.D.
preferre — *proffer, put forward for acceptance*, I. II. 306.
prerogatives — *airs of eminence*, II. II. 21.
President (with cap.) — *sitting member of Court*, I. I. 23, I. II. 6, 303; also at I. II. 14, with pun on:
president — *precedent*, I. II. 198, II. I. 12, V. II. 392.
prevent — *forestall, anticipate*, I. I. 79, I. II. 20, IV. II. 35; *hinder*, III. I. 108.
prune — *preen, trim*, III. I. 310.
puncto, in — *exact*, IV. I. 25.
punctuall — *punctilious*, IV. I. 38.
purles — *tucks or folds of a ruff*, II. II. 79.

qu — *cue*, III. I. 64.
quality — *rank, accomplishments*, IV. II. 16.
quick — *alive*, I. II. 201.
quirpo — (*Sp.* cuerpo) *undress clothes*, II. II. 102.

recent — *fresh*, II. I. 21.
reforme — *put right*, II. II. 83.
rellish — *suggestion, flavour*, II. II. 210, III. I. 22, 25.

sable — *black*, I. I. 69.
scruple — *the least part*, I. I. 107.
scutchion — *escutcheon, shield bearing coat-of-arms*, II. I. 50 S.D.
searecloth — *cere-cloth, winding-sheet*, II. I. 89.
seene — *versed*, III. I. 315.
shrewdly — *grievously*, III. I. 44.
simily — *simile*, II. I. 54.
slid — *by God's eyelid (an oath)*, II. I. 112.
'slight — *by God's light (an oath)*, II. I. 116.

slight	*slighting, contemptuous*, II. II. 186.
speed	*succeed*, IV. II. 224.
spittle	*hospital, hence, diseased*, III. I. 244.
spleene	*caprice, waywardness*, I. I. 64.
state	*estate*, IV. IV. 206, V. II. 276.
submisse	*submissive*, I. I. 216.
sudden	*very soon*, III. I. 42.
suddenly	*immediately*, IV. I. 184.
synonima	*synonymous*, V. I. 37.
take	*captivate*, I. II. 231.
tire-woman	*dressing-maid, responsible for clothes*, III. I. 67.
took up	*raised, borrowed*, I. I. 56.
touching	*concerning*, III. I. 496, V. II. 92.
toyes	*whims*, III. I. 524.
toyles	*snares*, I. I. 199.
traveld	*laboured (possibly with subsidiary meaning, travelled)*, III. I. 321.
turn'd	*fashioned*, II. II. 73.
tythe	*take one-tenth of*, V. I. 113.
uncivill	*ill-bred*, III. I. 576.
unconscionable	*extortionate, harsh*, V. I. I.
uncourtly	*impolite, lacking in knowledge of manners*, III. I. 192, V. II. 312.
vails	*perquisites, tips*, V. I. 97.
want	*lack*, I. I. 91, II. II. 20, V. II. 325; *falling-short*, IV. IV. 39; *need*, V. II. 10.
weede, weedes	*clothes*, II. I. 63, II. II. 84; *(with pun on) weed*, I. I. 178.
went for	*was assumed to be*, III. I. 32.
wherligig	*a whipping-top*, II. II. 19.
wittoll	*a complaisant cuckold*, V. II. 250.